# WOMEN

# OF

# MONGOLIA

# WOMEN
## OF
# MONGOLIA

MARTHA
AVERY

PUBLISHED BY ASIAN ART & ARCHAEOLOGY

IN ASSOCIATION WITH UNIVERSITY OF WASHINGTON PRESS

*for Sarah Binford Avery*

PHOTO CREDITS:
John Avery, page 45
John Stevenson, pages 35, 41, 65, 93, 97, 108, 141
Martha Avery, all others

Published by Asian Art & Archaeology
   600 Kalmia, Boulder, CO 80304
   email: mongolia@halcyon.com

Distributed in the United States of America and Canada
   by the University of Washington Press
   PO BOX 50096, Seattle, WA, 98145–5096
   email: uwpord@u.washington.edu

Library of Congress cataloguing-in-publication data
Avery, Martha, 1951–
   Women of Mongolia / Martha Avery.
         p.      cm.
   ISBN: 937321-05-2
      1. Women—Mongolia—Case studies.   I. Title.
HQ1765.8.A94             1996
305.4'0951'7—DC20                        96-22277
                                         CIP

Printed and bound in Hong Kong

# CONTENTS

## PREFACE

In this book, Mongolian women tell their stories. A street sweeper, an ambassador, a camel herder, and others talk about their lives.

A beautiful young woman gives her recipe for marmot, the staple food for the first seven years of her life. A herder describes how she gets water in winter—by chipping river ice and melting it over a dung fire. An anthropologist talks about her work in bone-DNA analysis.

The women whose lives appear here could be viewed as 'city women' and 'country women,' except that many of them fall in between. Mongolia is a country in transition. Mongolian women are affected by the great themes of the nation's current history: the transformation of a socialist structure to a market economy, from client state to independent country (and the hardships accompanying the loss of Russian subsidies), the great migration from the countryside to city. Distinctions between city and countryside are in flux. Rather than being grouped according to a one-dimensional contrast, these stories have been grouped into subject areas that unite them.

Mongolia is undergoing extreme and fundamental change, but underlying that change is a tenacious sense of tradition and continuity. Continuity is one of the primary themes of this book.

A second theme that unites these women is their willingness to change, and their desire to be an active agent of change through higher education. These are not the passive poor, buffeted by the winds of ill fortune, but strong, vigorous women who accept challenge. Self-reliance has always been a necessary condition of life on the steppe, and this habit of mind has not stopped at the city gates. To many women, self-reliance now means a higher education and a profession.

Resourcefulness and resilience form a third, more general theme, and are what struck me first when I began to meet Mongolian women. I did not set out to write a book about women; I am in Mongolia for other reasons. But as women described their lives, I began to realize that their stories should be written down. The positive, sturdy approach to life of these individuals is inspirational.

Naturally, there are also contrasts among these women. A liberal politician who may run for President of the country holds different views from a tractor driver whose hero is Lenin. The ambassador and the street sweeper see life from different perspectives. But all these women share a quality that begins to define itself as their stories are told.

* * *

Mongolia is an independent, democratic country situated between Russia and China, north of the Chinese province known as Inner Mongolia. Until the dissolution of the Soviet Union, Mongolia functioned as a part of the USSR. In March, 1990, the Communist Party stepped down and the country began a bloodless transition to a new government and a new economy.

There are only 2.4 million people living in Mongolia, in an area that is the size of western Europe. About 35 percent of the population now lives in the capital city of Ulaanbaatar, which lies at the southern edge of the forest zone, the Siberian taiga. Three main geographic zones stretch across the country: rolling hills and larch forests in the north, grassland or steppe in the middle, and gobi or gravelled semi-desert in the south.

Weather conditions in Mongolia are extreme. Winter temperatures hover between thirty to forty degrees below zero. The country sits on a high, exposed plateau—as one travels north and moves down in elevation to southern Siberia, the weather gets warmer, not colder. Historically, the buffer of the Gobi in the south and the shortness of the growing season in the rest of the country have preserved a uniquely Mongolian lifestyle.

For decades preceding 1990, Mongolia's economy was supported by the Soviet Union. The country benefited by a high rate of literacy and a fairly extensive health-care system. Many Mongolians were sent to Budapest, East Berlin, Prague, Sophia, Moscow, St. Petersburg, and other socialist cities for their higher education. Many speak both Russian and English and are highly cosmopolitan.

Some of these interviews were therefore conducted in English. When women did not speak English, I used an interpreter. Readers will note references to archaeology in several of the interviews—trips around the country were often to visit archaeological sites, and the accompanying geologist, Altangerel, and archaeologist, Batsaikhan, helped by serving as interpreters.

I want to express my appreciation to two women in particular, who interpreted for me and who introduced me to their friends. These were Gereltuya and Erdenechimeg. Gereltuya got this book started and Erdenechimeg kept it going. Thankyou.


Martha Avery
Ulaanbaatar, 1996

DIFFERENT PERSPECTIVES

RECIPE FOR MARMOT: *Inkhe*

First, of course, you have to shoot the marmot through the head. Otherwise you put holes in his skin and it doesn't work. Once you've got him, you open the mouth and take out all the innards. Yes, with your hand, through his mouth. If you use some kind of tool you might break the skin inside and that would spoil him. You must take the stomach out immediately once he's dead, or he will bloat.

Then you get some river rocks and heat them in the fire. We use a wood stove, so you just put the rocks in the coals. They have to be river rocks because mountain rocks split in the heat. River rocks don't split. Choose ones that are about the size of an egg, but flat rather than round.

Heat the rocks for around two hours, until they are red hot. Then put them inside the marmot, where the stomach was. Once they're inside, put the marmot on the coals of a very hot fire—not a flaming fire but one that has cooked down to hot coals. Leave the head on and the feet and fur and all. Just put him on top of the fire. The rocks cook him from the inside and the fire cooks him from the outside. Turn him occasionally. Cook for around two hours.

Gradually, you will see your marmot getting bigger and bigger. He puffs up with the heating, and finally you'll feel that he's about ready.

Take him off the fire and remove the stones. These stones are very therapeutic, so you can use them. Hold them in your hands, or sit on them, or put them under your feet. For example, if you have stomach problems, put them on top of your stomach for a while. The stones will be black and oily. Don't wash them off!

The first thing you can eat is the soup. Just a little; it's very strong. The soup has collected inside, and you can generally get two or three cups. Share it—a little bit for everyone.

Then you eat the meat.

Usually, when you eat an animal the shoulder blade is the choicest piece. It goes to the head of the family, who cuts the meat off this bone and divides it. The bone, called the *dal,* is quite small in a marmot, only around four inches long by two inches wide. It is small, but very *chic,** very special.

When I was young, until I was seven years old, I ate nothing but meat in the winter and dairy products in the summer. I lived with my grandparents in the countryside and marmot was one of our staples.

You can cook marmot many ways, not just with stones inside. You can freeze the meat and eat it later, dry it, boil it. You can also clean and cook the stomach. First cut it with scissors into small pieces, then stir it up with some herbs, salt and spices. This recipe is called *yalbig* in Mongolian.

We still eat a lot of marmot. My father had thirteen brothers and sisters, nine of whom are living. My mother has six brothers and sisters who are living, so there are a lot of aunts and uncles to visit in the countryside. We go out and eat marmot all summer long.

Of course we are forbidden to bring marmot into the city. It could bring plague and the whole city could get sick.* We call marmot plague *tarvagan takhal.* But people do bring marmots in nonetheless. They hide them in cars, in buses. I've even seen them hide a marmot in the exhaust pipe of a truck.

Mongolians are crazy about marmot. Maybe for foreigners it's not so tasty, but if you're used to it, well, it's probably like coffee for you. A strange taste when you have it first, but then you grow to like it.

When there's plague around, there are checkpoints throughout the countryside—police checking vehicles. The season for hunting marmot runs from August 15 to October 15. Just two months. Generally this is the time when plague is unlikely. After mid-October the marmots start hibernating.

Before the middle of August is the dangerous time for plague. The worst is in June, when the animals are still thin and weak from winter hibernation. But that time is also just when people are hungry too, and when they get to thinking a lot about eating marmot.

Plague only gets started when a marmot has been wounded, say by a dog, and retreats into its hole to die. There it infects the other marmots underground. So you don't want to injure a marmot if you're hunting. You want to kill him.

There are many medicinal uses of marmots. Marmot oil is good if you have burned your skin: it heals the burn quickly and with no infection. Also, if you have arthritis, just after killing the marmot you should wrap the warm skin around wherever it is you hurt most. The skin should be warm when you apply it, as warm as when the animal was alive. You wrap it tightly around your feet, say, and then let it stay there for two or three days. By that time, the marmot skin is stinking and green. When you take it off, you'll find you have no more illness. That's our traditional treatment.

Similarly, if you have a problem with your left kidney, you eat part of the left kidney of the marmot, raw. Just swallow it down. Same with the right kidney. And you can dry the pancreas and keep it for many years, using it whenever you need it. Just add some water and it's effective again.

Good luck!

* *Inkhe's own word for the dal is chic. She speaks in English, with a slight European accent. She is twenty years old, and is married to a German-French film director.*

* *The Black Plague of fourteenth-century Europe is believed to have come from Mongolia.*

### STREET SWEEPER: *Narmanda*

Yes, I am a street sweeper. You see my broom. Please, sit here on the curb with me while we speak.

My name is Narmanda* and I come from Arkhangai *aimag.** I came to Ulaanbaatar after graduation from the eighth grade—I was fourteen years old and from then on I have had no more schooling.

Now I'm 31. I'm married. My husband's first wife died, so he has two children from before and we have had three together. That's five children we provide for.

Sweeping? I started this job two months ago. I feel fortunate to have it; some friends found it for me. Before, I worked as a cleaning lady in a hospital. You know, with no higher education I couldn't hope to get a better job. I live in Bayiin Hosho, in the gertown on the edge of Ulaanbaatar. But I don't live in a *ger;** my house is made of wood.

My salary is 13,000 *tugriks** per month [$26].* If I work hard, then I'll get a bonus and the salary may be raised to 20,000 tugriks per month. I want you to know that 13,000 is the average salary for a street sweeper, it's not on the low side. I am supervised by the Amgalant District's Sanitation Department. There are thirty street sweepers working for our department, and it's one of many in Ulaanbaatar. Each sweeper is responsible for one stretch of road, the distance between one bus stop and the next. My stretch is on the main road from Amgalant to Ulaanbaatar.

All the brooms and clothes we use are provided by the Sanitation Department. Most people think that the hardest time is in winter. Maybe so—the temperature does go down to forty below zero. But I know personally that summer and autumn are pretty difficult. What do I sweep up? Mostly wrappers, papers, cigarette butts, plus the general dirt. Right now, of course, are the nut shells. You can see the nut vendors on every corner, a bag in front of them full of those pine nuts. People are scouring the mountains for the nuts. Anything to sell, and anything to eat. For me, it's a headache.

What do my children do? My youngest son stays at home, alone. He's only four years old, but he understands the difficulties his parents are

having. They have to go to work. No, I've never been to any women's organization to ask for help. I know there are such places—I've heard about them on radio and TV. But I haven't tried.

Before the market economy started, four years ago, my salary was enough to get by on. The main reason was that food prices were lower, so my children, who were smaller then, got enough to eat. I'm not well educated—I can't do any of these small private enterprises they talk about on my own. So I decided that the only possibility for me was to work with my hands. My work starts at eight o'clock in the morning. Lunch is from twelve to two, then I work again from two to six o'clock. On Saturday I work half a day. On Sunday I can rest.

I take the bus to get to work. I ride for around forty minutes each way, but of course there's also waiting time for the bus on either end. I don't mind that. This is a good job, and I hope to be able to do it for some years. I just hope that I can keep healthy and work hard, because then I can qualify for a bonus. The Sanitation Department helps with wood and charcoal for fuel in the winter—a wooden house is colder than a ger. Sometimes they give a New Year's bonus.

My plan is to do only this job, and to do it well. I hope to do it until pension age, which will be for another fifteen or twenty years. I am afraid I couldn't find another job.

What do I think about the government, and this whole political process? I'm not interested in politics. My husband is forty-one, ten years older than I. He works as a driver for the state film company and his salary is 16,000 tugriks [$32]. He's a good man; he never beats me. But he likes to drink—I have to say that he drinks a little too much *arkhi.*

Mostly, I worry about my daughters. If a girl can get a good education, she'll be all right. I would be glad if my daughters could learn any kind of profession.

A woman must, first of all, be educated. I realize that, because I myself am hampered by lack of training. I can't get into business because I don't have the knowledge of how to start. If my daughters get jobs in the future and have their own income, they can spend it on their own health, for example. They won't have to rely on a husband's money to survive.

The main problem is health. Medical service is bad here. I have a medical services book; everyone has one now. Nonetheless, doctors look at my face and know what kind of work I do. So service is bad. In fact there is really no medical treatment at all.

But I am optimistic—I understand that an unqualified woman can't find other work. My daughters will do better. That is my hope.

*Her name means 'sun's rays' in Mongolian.*

*An aimag is the Mongolian equivalent of a state or province.*

*Tugriks are the Mongolian currency.*

*All exchange rates in this book use the 1996 rate of around five hundred tugriks to one US dollar.*

*This is the Mongolian word for 'yurt,' a felt house. Gertowns are shantytowns with wooden shacks as well as gers.*

*Arkhi is the word for Mongolian vodka.*

AMBASSADOR: *Baljinnyam*

Professionally, I have been a diplomat. I spent thirty years in the Foreign Ministry. Among other posts, I was Ambassador and Permanent Representative to the United Nations Office in Geneva. I suppose my friends call me the first female Ambassador in the country.

My responsibilities in Geneva included representation at all the international organizations in Europe, the FAO [Food and Agriculture Organization] in Italy, and so on. I enjoyed it. The Ambassadorial post was my second assignment in Geneva—I'd been there the first time in 1969, when my husband and I opened the office together.

How did I start this career? After I graduated from the Mongolian National University, they wanted me to stay on as a professor. That was in 1963. But the Foreign Ministry also wanted me, so I joined the Ministry—and kept on working in foreign affairs until 1992. Most people were not trained in Moscow back then. Our Mongolian National University produced many well-known scientists and scholars. It was a very fine university in those days. In recent years young people have been sent to be educated in Moscow, but back then it was rare.

Lately I have been involved in women's issues—I have just returned from the Women's Forum in Beijing. I am concerned right now about who in Mongolia will spearhead the implementation of the 'Platform of Action.' This is a problem. There is no mechanism within Mongolia to take real action. There is a small office in the Ministry of Labor in charge of women's affairs. It's staffed by only one or two women, and such an office can't really do anything at all. They have immense problems to deal with and absolutely no budget. So we first have to create a mechanism for accomplishing results.

As you may know, there are perhaps twenty women's organizations in Mongolia. I don't know the exact number, there are probably more —in short, too many. The effort gets fragmented. People don't know what is being done. We need a coordinating body or we need to consolidate these groups. The government plans to hold a conference early next year, to discuss these things. But frankly speaking, there is no government policy at all on women.

I have received many complaints from women who are unable to get access to credit or loans. There is no facility for dealing with the crisis that the transition to a market economy has created. You may have heard of the Mongolian Women's Federation, an organization that is over seventy years old. Younger critics say it is too old. On the other hand, it is the only organization with any kind of material basis for action. It has a council in every aimag, it has a special radio program, a magazine, a newspaper.

Is the money for the Federation going into the wrong hands, getting lost? Interesting question. No, I believe the Federation is dealing with its funds responsibly. They have a revolving fund in every aimag. They are implementing good projects, through the Asia Fund, the Australian government, and so on. But the overall situation in terms of women's organizations in Mongolia is bad. Women should be clear about their objectives and then set out to accomplish them. The goal we all have is the same. Criticising one another gives a very bad impression to others. People say, "So many groups, always criticizing each other. What's the use?"

The government should take the initiative, yes. But they need to work closely with NGOs [non-governmental organizations] to get things done. The government does not have the capability to do the job itself. And things badly need to get done.

*Regarding a reported $100 million being given to poverty alleviation, most of which is targeted at women and children: where does it all go?*

Not only $100 million. More. Other aid projects too—the amount of money coming into Mongolia is enormous.* And where indeed does it go. American aid for example. They say they are supporting the power station, but where has all that money gone?

*What accountability is there? What kind of monitoring, and ways to measure progress?*

For the last thirty years, governments around the world had so many platforms, so many proposals. In the end, it was difficult to know if there had in fact been any progress. We now want our government to stand by its promises. To say, in concrete terms, for example, 'the number of women involved in decision-making processes will increase to a specific percent by the year 2000.' We want the government to show that it has not only made a commitment but has implemented specific plans. The government must now be accountable to the people.

*For thirty years, you were 'the government.' Now you are criticizing the government. How do you feel about that?*

Yes, I used to be 'government.' Before. Now, although I am not part of any organization with an anti-government agenda, not part of an NGO for instance, I have a very mixed impression of government. As a government representative at UN meetings, attending so many sessions, of course we always looked down on NGOs. They talked too much. They were always criticizing us.

Now I am not government. And I am just now coming to realize things. If you go to the countryside and see how it is, you know more about real life. Governments are too high—as we say, they're up there in the sky. They like to pick up just a little information and use it, saying, "You see, things are good. We are making great progress."

Especially in these last few years, this is no longer the case. There have been great changes in the country. And this women's movement has really come out as a result. Before, you did not see beggars in the streets. Everybody, even if they were poor, had something to eat. Education was paid for, so people did not worry so much about their childrens' futures. Now, everyone is concerned. They wonder, what will happen tomorrow?

It's good to have these women's organizations emerge. They're needed. Before, in official forums, I had to follow the line, which is why I was so impressed at Beijing. The forum was so free. For me it was really something extraordinary. I went from one seminar to another, listening to all the discussions. Arabs were talking about their issues, Latin Americans were speaking Spanish, and Africans mostly French, but you could still get something out of it. People were talking.

Russians were, of course, discussing the problem of countries in transition. And this is our problem. The transition is having an enormous impact on women. Also, they were discussing ethnic problems, which fortunately we don't have yet, although it is looming in the future. I mean Moslems.

*What is the population growth rate now? 2.9%?*

No, the rate is no longer 2.9%. It has gone down to 2.5, maybe 2.4%. The peak was in the 1970s, and the rate has been declining since 1980. In the last few years in particular, women have been having fewer children as an attempt to survive economically. Yes, legalizing abortions has accelerated the trend. Legal abortions are a good thing on the one hand, but harmful in some ways. Very young girls are having abortions now.

*After years as a high government official in a socialist system, did you feel any psychological trauma in switching to a new sort of mentality?*

No, for me there was no trauma at all. Perhaps because I had been abroad for so many years. Things were clear to us on the outside; we understood the problems of both socialist and capitalist systems. We could see the good and bad things in both. It was no surprise to see the end of a system which didn't work, and so I personally have felt no emotional trauma as policy switched to a market economy.

Many old people, however, have felt enormous trauma. They had this ideal, working for socialism all their lives, working hard for a better life for their children. They never expected that at the end of it there would be absolutely nothing at all. First, no way to support themselves, materially. Then the added insult of being told by young people, 'You are nothing. You were wrong. Go away.'

The change was overnight. It was too strong, this wrench, too extreme. People are settling down now, and even the young are recognizing the realities of the situation. But especially in 1992–93, people were really hit hard.

*What about the change in foreign relations, given the disintegration of the Soviet Union?*

We older people worry about China. You know, for many decades we were able to play the China card against the Russians, and the Russian card against the Chinese. We could always say to China, the Russians will come and teach you a lesson. Now it's hard. Big powers have their own national interests. Older Mongolians know the Chinese very well, indeed they know too well. We have only some two million people here, in this vast country. We have had to learn how to preserve our identity. In past centuries we had an unwritten law: Mongolian nobles do not marry Chinese. The Manchus had this rule too, but were less successful in remaining Manchu. Look at the Manchus now: gone. They lost their country, and even their own language, although they once ruled all of China.

In Mongolia we now have an 'open policy' toward China. We are all very friendly with each other. But I can remember that my father always used to say, "Don't Trust China." Why, Poppa? I would ask him. "One day," he would say, "they will come and sit here in the seat of honor, as owners."

I keep that in mind. The Chinese will not come openly, with weapons. Nobody will realize they are here. The Australians, the Japanese come and make big news out of their investments. Not the Chinese. They just get it done quietly. Young people don't know this. They don't know the history.

My home aimag is Bayanhongor. I was born in Ulaanbaatar, but spent most of my first eighteen years in the countryside. So yes, you could say I am a country girl from a herder's family. I love the steppe. When I go there, I feel free. My husband is from the same aimag. I go back every year: first you have to go to the aimag capital, and then by bus to the village; then you ride a horse out into the countryside to my relatives. My uncle's children still live there.

My own children don't feel the same way, unfortunately. They were raised in cities and had a Russian education. Everywhere we went, they were required to attend the Soviet mission's school. But I went to the countryside just before the Women's Forum and took my grandchildren. I was pleased to see that they had a wonderful time.

---

*\* Mongolia is currently the highest per capita recipient of international aid of any country in the world.*

*This cleaning-lady sweeps the stairwells of the building in which Baljinnyam lives and is the type of woman she talks about in this interview. Stairwells in city buildings are often full of urine and excrement, especially in winter, when the homeless stay in them to try to stay warm. This lady never misses a day of work.*

CONTINUITY

BY THE MOUNTAINS: *Manduhai*

*L*ooking for petroglyphs in the Tevsh Mountains, we come across a *ger nestled at the foot of the steep, rocky hillside.*

Welcome! Please come in. Have a seat.

*The sitting arrangement in a ger is specific. A woman sits on the left side as you face south, a man on the right. The door of a ger always faces south. The lady of the house generally stays by the central hearth, near the door, tending the fire, pouring tea.*

My husband and I can show you the petroglyphs. I have lived in this area all my life and I know these mountains well. The Tevsh mountains and the Arts Bogd across the way are ancient. We don't know when people did the drawings, or when those stone graves outside the ger were built—certainly a long time ago.

Yes, we take care of the graves. Like an *ovoo,** they are sacred, so we keep the stones in order. There are so many graves along this ridge of mountains—we just tend the ones right here by our home.

This is our winter place. We moved here one week ago, the third week in October. We haven't been coming here for too many years....I am twenty-two and my husband is twenty-three. *Proudly, she glances at a fat, healthy child sleeping on the bed.*

Please have tea! This is made with camel's milk. Everything we eat is from camels at this time of year—and this is camel's-milk *airak.** Very healthy. This is *aral* and this is *shartos.** They say camel's milk has the highest percentage of protein and vitamins.

The camels are over beyond that hill right now, out eating. One of my family is tending them. My family comes from this area and is scattered around. Mostly on the northern side of the valley. You find the graves on the northern slopes, too, facing south—this place catches the sun in the winter and you can look south across the valley. For thousands of years, nobody would think of facing north! Outside there, you see the Arts Bogd Range.

I am told that the Arts Bogd is one of the great archaeological sites in Mongolia. Americans came here years ago,* and later Russians and Mongolians—they look for what we call *tengeriin cholon,** stone tools made by early man. Down there to the west, where you see the end of the Arts Bogd Range, they found truck-loads of them at an ancient workshop. Just out on top of the earth. The Tevsh Mountains have these things as well. In the past, when I was a child, archaeologists came to study these mountains. Not so many in the last five years.

There are two main kinds of graves here along this slope. One is a mound of large stones, like the one to the west of our ger. The other has a square border of stones around a mound. We don't know what it means. They are both meant to be bronze-age graves.

I like to think of those people also looking out across this valley. We have a saying in Mongolian, *'Erhuni jargal, idsugui heer.'* Man's joy is in wide open, empty spaces. Every Mongolian believes this.

No, life is not really solitary. In fact, we have a good network of communication. Perhaps because we rely on each other, living in the open like this. We aren't isolated.

Many of the petroglyphs are of animals. Some are like me, like mothers. Come, I'll show you. *She smiles, then leads us outside.*

*These two, man and wife, have an old-world kind of formality. The manner in which countryside people greet each other is a stylized ritual. There are specific greetings for each different season, there are ways of approaching a ger, ways of entering, ways of sitting.*

*'Civilization' is like a thin spiderweb of these traditions, spread over a large area. Given the tenuous nature of life, the traditions or connecting threads are important and consequently tenacious.*

*This couple is like an extension of the mountains, like the bedrock of the Tevsh Range. In many respects, their lives are a continuation of ancient ways.*

*A typical bronze-age grave dating from the first millenium* BC, *on the slopes of the Tevsh Mountains in Bayanhongor aimag.*

*An ovoo is a mound of rocks, built and maintained to honor the spirits.*

*Airak is the Mongolian name for fermented mare's milk.*

*These are various dried milk products.*

*The Andrews Expedition traveled through Mongolia in the years 1922–28.*

* *Tengeriin cholon means 'sky stone.' Worked stones are also sometimes described as 'pencil stones,' since the flaking on all sides sometimes makes the remaining core look like a pencil.*

BY THE RIVER: *Myagmarsuren*

*M*yagmarsuren is a strong woman, with unusually thick, short hair that stands up straight, on its own, like the cropped mane of a Mongolian pony.

*Her ger is on the flat ground east of the Egiin Gol,* before the hills rise to the east. Rich grassland surrounds it. An outside kitchen is set up as a place to make milk products and grind grain. Three homemade carts with wooden wheels stand outside, one with a large water barrel on it.*

*The setting is beautiful. It is the period known as 'altan namar,' golden autumn. Larch trees have turned the hillsides brilliant yellow; white trunks of birch trees show through the mixed taiga forest. The sky is blue, the river is wide.*

I was born here, in the Egiin Gol valley. I have lived here all my life. My husband was also born in this valley, and my twelve children were born at home, in our ger. I'm forty-two.

We are getting ready to move to our winter home soon. We'll go in around seven or eight days, put all our belongings on the carts you see outside. Once we get to Bituugiin Tsagaan, putting up the ger again will take around fifty minutes. We move four or five times a year, so the process is familiar.

Our winter home is not far from here. It's between those hills to the northeast, a wide area between two streams that gives protection from the wind but still has grass and water for the animals. Bituugiin Tsagaan means 'enclosed white place.' The word for white, tsagaan, has a special meaning for us, hallowed or sacred. The place has been used by our ancestors for a very long time. Our archaeologist friend here says the graves in Bituugiin Tsagaan date from 2,500 years ago. There are nine major tombs. We spend the winter just to the west of them, in a grove of old trees.

What do I do all day? There's plenty to do! First, I get up at around six o'clock in the morning to milk the cows. My daughter helps me. We have nineteen cows to milk, so it takes around one hour.

After that, I do various other jobs. I go to bed around ten or eleven in

*Myagmarsuren in her outdoor kitchen. Dairy products dry on the sun-roof above her, protected from hungry birds by a dangling dead magpie.*

the evening. We make everything here. Yes, the wheels of the carts outside are an example. My husband makes them, out of wood. We use the carts to move the ger and our belongings. They are pulled by oxen. I make all the ropes, out of horsehair—you can see them on the outside of the ger, holding down the felt.

Then there is always food to be prepared for the winter. This bag, made from a cow's hide, is for our airak. We have many mares and we milk them every two hours. The fresh milk is poured in here. No, we don't boil it first. We boil the cow's milk for making *tarakh,** but not the airak. This wooden plunger is put in the bag and pummelled up and down—it must be done a minimum of two thousand times. The way to make airak is described in our *Secret History of the Mongols,** so the tradition has been the same for a long time.

You should drink more airak! A guest should drink at least three times. You've noticed—it's stronger now, in the autumn. That's because the grass the mares eat is richer, full of nutrients. The strongest and best airak is just before the weather turns really cold.

Mares generally stop giving milk in November. For the winter months, we distil cow's milk to make a drink called *shimiin arkhi.* We're making it every day now, for the cold winter months. It's best when it's just warm and fresh—have some!

In the autumn, another thing I do during the day is grind the grain. We grow *har boda* in a valley up to the north. The name means 'black rice.' Here, this is it. Round like millet, but a shiny black color. I take the husks off with that wooden mallet outside. I'll show you.

The large square hunk of wood is for weight on top, it's not the pounder. The pounding part is the round handle. It takes some energy to keep lifting it up and down. We plant the har boda in May, and harvest it in September. I use the flour to make a kind of fried pancake in the winter.

You can't see them now, because they're out in the hills, but we also have around two hundred sheep. My children and husband herd them. I don't do that. But the sheep start lambing in February and March, so that is a busy time of the year for me. We have to find each newly born animal and make sure it is protected and survives. We often bring them into the ger to keep them warm.

*Myagmarsuren pounding har boda, 'black rice,' to remove the husks. She harvests the har boda in the fall and it serves as the main grain for her family through the winter.*

We get water every two days from the river—hitch up the oxen and pull the cart down there. In the winter, we get ice and melt it over the fire. Of course we first have to collect the dung to make the fire. We do that all summer, in preparation for the cold.

So there is plenty to do. I still like to embroider. I did the pillows with the peacocks and strawberries on them. Peacocks are symbolic of course, but other than that we don't have an altar here. There is a shrine out back, made of large upright stones. One has Sanskrit characters on it. It's not a grave, it's what we call a *manjilo*. The monastery in the valley to the east was destroyed in the 1930s. We don't keep Buddhist objects or *sutras*\* here, but...well, we have our traditions. Who knows what they should be called. For example, at Bituugiin Tsagaan there are ancient trees surrounding our home. Two of them are sacred, and I put a rope around their trunks, with cloth streamers. I do it to respect the gods that live there.

Then there are things we do to make sure the home is safe and well. For example, the saw up there above the door, tucked under the wooden poles: that is to make sure no evil person comes through that door. Also, the rope hanging from the middle wooden piece at the center of the ger: we wind that under the wooden poles in the shape of a wolf's snout. If any evil comes in, the spirit of the wolf will take care of it. I don't know if we believe it, but we still do it.

Right now, around twenty families live in the Egiin Gol valley. You can't see any from here—the valley runs for miles, so there's plenty of land. Our families have been here as long as anyone can remember. We live well. Life involves a lot of work, but life is good.

*There are plans to flood the Egiin Gol valley in order to build a hydro-electric power plant. Some scientists believe that the dam is unnecessary and will be an ecological disaster. Lake Hovsgol is the source of the river and Lake Baikal is its final destination.*

*Making milk tea, which is a combination of brick tea, rich milk, and salt.*

*\*Gol means 'river' in Mongolian.*

*\*Tarakh is the Mongolian word for yogurt.*

*\*The Secret History of the Mongols is the first book known to have been written in the Mongolian language. It was written some 750 years ago.*

*\*A sutra is a Buddhist scripture.*

### SOUTH OF TUVA: *Yak herder*

*right: Mongolian cheese is squeezed between rocks, as shown here, to remove as much moisture as possible. Drying is the main way to preserve food until the deep freeze of winter sets in.*

*below: Yaks provide the main source of milk in this northern part of Mongolia, due south of the fabled land of Tuva. Yak milk is made into a particularly rich and delicious yogurt. This family eats mainly yak products during the summer.*

*These are yak-milk products drying in the sun. Each variety and shape of 'cheese' has a different name. These protein-rich nuggets will be dried until they are rock hard and can be preserved through the winter.*

*Handmade wooden wheels are common on northern carts. Carts like this are generally used to move house, when the ger is disassembled and taken to a different place. They are also used to carry water in barrels from the nearest river.*

NEAR ERDENEZU: *Erdenechimeg*

*C*himge stands with her family before the Orkhon River, famous
*in Mongolian history. Behind her rise hills that hold one of*
*Mongolia's richest paleolithic sites. Chimge lives in the city, but knows*
*the countryside well. She understands the pressures that are forcing*
*women to move into the city.*

My goal is to start a shelter-house for women and children, a place
they can go together. We have a facility for homeless children, and
various support systems for mid-level women. We also certainly have
prisons for women. But Mongolia has no place where mothers and
children can stay together while they have the greatest need for help,
the greatest need for continuity in their lives.

Take the street sweepers we see everywhere, sweeping so hard all day.
If this kind of woman loses her job, she has nowhere to go. She can't
find another job and she quickly descends into destitution. Generally
the children are then sent out to beg on the streets, for the family. I've
seen it so many times now. Young children are often the only way the
family survives.

I particularly want to establish the sort of halfway house where young
unmarried mothers can go for advice. We have no counselling services in this country at all. Young mothers can sometimes give up
their children to the orphanage and hope to keep them alive that way,
but there must be a better way to counsel mothers and their children.

I plan to set up training programs for women as part of the facility.
Simply giving money, or shelter, is not enough. These women need
guidance in how to fend for themselves, how to survive in a market
economy. Many are not educated at all.

A variety of programs are being set up in Mongolia now for women
in the middle levels, women who are capable of running small enterprises. And, of course, there are substantial amounts of money coming into the country from foreign aid organizations.

It is perhaps an open secret that most of this money goes to men.

Until I had differences of opinion with the management, I worked in the Women's Federation. I saw what was happening behind the scenes. The xx Bank, to take only one case, was loaning up to two million tugriks per woman. The money was loaned to women, all right, but they were often wives of the big bosses in Mongolia. A simple woman could never hope to pay back the loan, so why give money to her!

A few loans have in fact been made for poverty alleviation, to poor women, but the funds are not accompanied by any kind of training or advice. A simple, uneducated woman has no idea how to pay back that money. What happens is a disgrace: at the end of the period the head of the Women's Federation prepares a list of the names of women who have failed to pay back their loans. They're then locked up. While I was at the Federation, eight women were sent to prison. I feel these women were unfairly pushed into prison. It is wrong to loan women money without making sure they have some idea of how to repay it. But the Mongolian institutions making the loans are interested in one thing: having a long list of women in order to show donors that they are doing their job. Foreigners don't know about this problem.

We need to make a realistic plan for giving credit. We shouldn't just give money and then go away, saying 'come back in two years with the money and interest.'

My husband works for the police. You know that. His job relates to white-collar crime, people who are taking state money. I don't object to the police, and I don't object to a system of justice. But pushing women into prison is the wrong way to raise their standard of living.

Mongolia has meetings and conferences on the subject of poverty alleviation all the time. The heads of Mongolian agencies take trips to foreign countries. Little of it has any direct impact on women's lives. By setting up a simple shelter and counselling center, I want to do it, not talk about it.

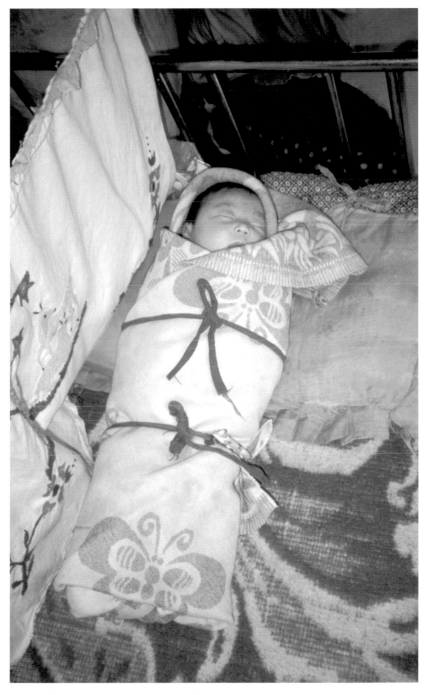

*Mongolian baby wrapped in the traditional manner.*

## COUNTRY TO CITY

### THE GREAT MIGRATION: *Camel lady*

Greetings! Yes, I can stop for a short time, but not for long—my herds and family are coming along behind. I'm in the lead with the camels; the others are following with the horses and sheep. We started in Omon Gov' aimag* two months ago. We're on our way to the city, to Ulaanbaatar.

Once we get there, we'll sell the animals and start city life!

Here they come—I'd better move along. Thankyou for the cigarette. Goodbye!

*Omon Gov' aimag is in the South Gobi, one of the poorest parts of Mongolia.*

*The flocks, being herded by husband and sons, are following behind. She is a mile or two ahead of them, leading the way with her two camels.*

*Laden with all the family's household belongings, her camels will be sold once they arrive in Ulaanbaatar.*

*Off to the big city, and a new life.*

MILK GIRLS: *Oyuntuya and Oyungerel*

*O*ur bus breaks down. We catch a lorry going our way, climb in the back, and jolt along in the cold wind. Then the lorry breaks down too. We walk. Standing by the road, in the middle of nowhere, are two lovely young girls carrying milk cans. They are walking slowly down the road, waiting for a bus to come along.

We are sisters. I'm fifteen, my sister is thirteen. I'm Oyuntuya. She's Oyungerel.

We're waiting for a bus to take us back to town. It's about fifteen kilometers from here. We've been up to that ger, over there, beyond those hills. We come here twice a week to pick up the milk.

We get it from the family of my mother's friend. We used to live around here. Milk in town costs 140 tugriks a liter. Coming out here, we get it free, and it's also more fresh. Usually we milk the cow ourselves. Today our mother's friend did it for us since we were late.

*The fifteen-year-old is chubby, with red cheeks; she looks rosy all over. The thirteen-year-old is slender and more reserved.*

I study English in school. I've studied for two years. We study English now, not Russian any more.

*Oyuntuya's accent is excellent and her smile is beautiful. When the bus finally comes, we climb aboard. It bounces on the potholes and the milk splashes on my trousers—with horrified glances at each other, they help brush it off. The fresh milk feels buttery to the touch.*

Bye!

*Cheerful again, they step down from the bus into the rapidly growing town, and head off carrying their milk cans to whatever life may hold.*

ON THE STEPPE: *Tsenden*

*T*he sun is setting on Tsenden's ger, on the steppe. She lives south of the southernmost edge of the Siberian taiga. Before her lie miles of grassland and rolling hills. Her mother is working on the ground outside, stitching old jackets together to make a new ger cover. Tsenden is getting cows ready for milking. When she sees us, she immediately invites us into her home.

*She is living both an urban and a rural life. She takes advantage of the steppe by raising animals: so far, the pastureland is free. She sells the milk and meat products in a small enterprise she runs in a nearby town.*

I am both. I am a traditional herder, but I also run a business in town. For part of the year I help with the animals, as you see. I make milk products and the meat that supports our enterprise. The rest of the year, I rent the kitchen at the Women's Council in Zunmod, where I make *booz** and *hoshoor** and sell them. We have fifty goats and sheep, six female horses for the airak, twenty male horses, and four cows.

*A commotion suddenly erupts outside. Bellowing cows sound as though they are charging the ger. Excusing herself, Tsenden rushes outside and the bellowing subsides. When she returns she explains that the calves were trying to get at the mother's milk.*

In the summertime, my cows give an average of twenty liters of milk a day. In the winter that goes down to ten liters per day. We milk each cow twice a day, and use the milk to make what you see here. This *urum* is a soft creamy pancakelike treat. We skim the cream off rich milk and dry it slightly. These *etsuji* are harder chunks of dried milk, and *aral* is the flat dried milk that you see drying on tops of gers.

We make these things all summer and then have them to eat in winter. Also, we have been making a lot of airak. We freeze it outside when cold weather comes, and at the time of *Tsagaan Sar,** we thaw it and drink it. It will be as fresh then as it is today.

We've been in this location on the steppe for twenty days. We'll move on to the winter location in mid-October but exactly when depends on the weather. The grass here is better for our animals, so we don't

*Tsenden, in the middle, is accompanied by two friends, Erdenechimeg on the left and Cholontsetseg on the right. Tsenden has put on her best del for the photograph.*

want to move too soon. The winter place is just up beyond those hills. We'll walk up later and you can see it in the distance. It takes less than a day to disassemble the ger, pack everything on our carts and move. My children all help.

What if some other herder is already in the place we would normally come to? We would simply look for another place. We would not get angry at whoever is there; we'd just find another way. Where we go depends on the grass. Sometimes, with more or less rain, it is necessary to move often. It really all depends on the weather and the snow and rainfall.

I have six children. In fact this is my son's ger, not mine. I am just now putting up a ger for myself in town, in Zunmod. I'm forty-three years old, and my oldest son and daughter-in-law have one child, so I'm a grandmother. I definitely feel that a big family is best. Larger is better. Right now, for instance, there are only four people here in this ger, and it feels lonely. I am accustomed to more life, more activity. It's better for children and better for the family to have many children.

How do I change clothes with all these people around? We have ways of doing things privately. We just turn our backs and use the *del** to conceal what is going on.

No, I'm certainly not a Buddhist. I believe in myself. My parents were not particularly religious either, just so-so. It wasn't terribly important. Of course, I do believe in all the things that Mongolian people normally believe in. The traditional things, not religion, that is. For example? Well, for example, belief in the mountains. Belief that one should not kill fish in the rivers. Belief in the fire of the hearth. That sort of thing.

Then there are things that we don't really believe in, but we go along with anyway, just in case. For example, the magic of animals. Crows in particular, and snakes, have ways of casting spells. Every schoolchild knows that a goose can break a man's stirrup if the man has done something bad to it.

Why a stirrup? Because the stirrup is so important. A person is immobile without it. When a man leaves on a long trip, we sprinkle milk on his stirrup.

Marmots? Oh yes, many stories about marmots. One must be careful to kill a marmot that has been shot. It is said, for example, that if you don't kill him outright when you shoot him, his squeal will put a curse on the hunter, and the hunter may die.

We also have traditions that you wouldn't call beliefs. For example, the calendar. There are days on which one is better off doing some things and better off not doing other things. You can see on this calendar that these days are good for cutting children's hair. We don't cut hair on days that are unlucky. We move only on a day that is a lucky day to move. People are very careful about this. Business negotiations are done only on auspicious days.

My business in town has been fairly successful so far. I don't pay rent for the kitchen, which helps. In exchange for being able to use it I keep the Women's Council building clean. It's hard to say what my monthly income is, since we earn very little some months, and then we may sell a cow another month. But I also get a pension from the government of 4,200 tugriks per month [$9].

The pension comes because I worked many years for the government, and also because I had six children. Before, we were given awards for having more children, and the pension system also rewarded mothers who had more children. If you worked twenty years for the government and also had more than five children, you were awarded a pension early. Now it may be different. In any event, I'm entitled to and do receive a pension.

I pick it up at the bank in town, right across from the post office. With the money from the pension, and also my earnings from the food business, I am able to buy things like rice, flour, and clothes for the children. I guess those are the main expenses.

I was a State Worker for many years. I left school after the fourth year in secondary school and then worked for seven years doing the milking on a state cow farm. We milked by hand all day.

Then I was the night watchman at the agricultural office. I did that for more than ten years. After that, I got the pension because of my children. My husband worked as an accountant in an office in town. When the change of government came he lost his job and mostly he just sits at home now. One of my children is older—the son who has the child. The others are all in school, and it is my hope that they will be fully educated. The one thing I worry about is the future of my children.

Out here in the countryside, they do most of the work. I am like the teacher—I instruct them. As winter comes, we butcher some animals and I use the meat in my booz and hoshoors. Right now we are using mainly mutton. As winter starts we will begin to use horse meat. One kilo of horse meat costs around 500 tugriks in the summer [$1]; right now it's only 400 tugriks since it's slaughtering season and there's so much mutton and beef on the market.

I was born in this aimag, in Baiyunjul sum. I've lived in this area all my life. In the future, I would hope that I can live here in the countryside with my animals. If the children want to stay with me, that's no problem. I hope they will. The only condition is that they must first finish school.

*Booz and hoshoor are the national foods of Mongolia; both are variations of meat wrapped in dough and boiled.*

*Tsagaan Sar is the Mongolian New Year's holiday, which is generally held some time in late January or February. The name means 'White Month.' White is a sacred and auspicious color for Mongolians.*

*A del is the wraparound robe worn by both men and women in Mongolia. Since it wraps around the body, it can be taken off without going over the head, and one can use it as a sort of screen.*

*Tsenden's mother is sewing old jackets together to make a cover for their ger. The shadow in front of her is thrown by a basket used for collecting dung. Behind is a small 'one-more ger,' a ger used just for storing things.*

ON THE OUTSKIRTS OF ULAANBAATAR: *Dewajao*

*D*ewajao wears a bright red kerchief around her head. We enter her
compound through a gate in the fence and she welcomes us into
her little domain. The home is in a gertown on the outskirts of
Ulaanbaatar. It is thirty minutes by tram from the center of the city.

Please come in! Welcome!

I am glad to tell you about myself. Yes, I live here, and this is my
house. We built it ourselves out of scrap wood and cement. In back is
the stable for the animals in winter, but I'll show you that later. Come
in, come in.

Where are the animals now? Out grazing! Most of the families in this
area keep animals, and we take turns herding them. My children go
with them sometimes, but not today. The animals go everywhere.*
We try to keep them out of the streets of course, but there are no
restrictions on where they should eat. Just out there.

*A geranium blooms in her window beside a healthy aloe plant. The door
and windows face east, not south, unlike the traditional arrangement of
a Mongolian home. She sits on a tiny stool, legs solidly spread.*

I get up at 5:30 and start the day getting milk from my cows. I use it to
make this tea. It's fresh. *She pours the milk tea into a Chinese porcelain
bowl.*

I have ten cows and three calves right now. In winter, for food, I buy
them two big lorries of hay. I keep it out back, in a building just for
the hay. We buy it in September and October, so we've been preparing it recently. Each bale of hay costs 350 tugriks, and each lorry car-
ries 280 bales, so one winter costs me 196,000 tugriks [almost $400].
That's the cheapest price you can get, by the way.

Four of my ten cows give milk. I do the milking myself but sometimes my children help. If they're busy I do it. Then we also have
quite a few sheep and forty goats. That's a lot of animals for here.

I have ten children. Three of them have families themselves now. The
other seven live here. Where do they sleep? Right here on the floor!

Some sleep in a summer building out back. My husband and I take those two beds.

Yes, this is my husband. *He has come in and taken a position sitting on the floor. He sits with one knee up, one down, in the traditional posture of Mongolian nomads. By custom, the knee facing the door is always up, the other down. This is meant to make it easier to scramble out of the door when you have to move fast. Since a man sits on the west side of a ger, his right knee is always up. This husband sits in a new wooden house, but maintains the proper way of sitting in a ger.*

Has life changed in the last few years? It was easier before. Now it's hard, and hardest of all for old people. But my family eats every day. We're not the kind that has to say, 'we go two days without eating for every day that we eat.'

*Dewajao offers semi-dried cream skimmed from the top of rich milk. One always takes at least a pinch of what is offered in a Mongolian household. To refuse would be impolite, even if the family can scarcely afford to feed itself.*

My two oldest children work as government employees, a third boy is now in the army, and a fourth graduated from secondary school last year and is looking for a job—he'll probably become a driver. Two of my daughters work in a factory making clothes. Three more children are still in school. I have six daughters and four boys, and I'm proud of my children. Everyone knows what to do. They are busy all day.

*The house is in the old Russian style, with a Russian stove that separates a kitchen area from the main room. There is no dividing wall; the house is one big room. Door frames are painted blue, the walls white. At the northern end of the room, between the two beds, is a little shrine.*

Those two sutras* on the altar table belonged to my father. Both of our fathers were lamas. That portrait is of my husband's grandfather. That's a photograph of the Dalai Lama.

*Three modern, grotesquely fat ceramic Buddhas adorn the shrine, next to an ancient white conch.* A thanka* in a wooden frame is adjacent to a miniature Beefeater's Gin bottle. The objects of devotion are a mixture of kitsch and antiques.*

Every morning, first thing, I put a spoonful of tea in this cup, and some bread and yogurt here on the altar. After a day or two, when it's not as fresh, I put it in the stove—not outside where animals can get it. I burn it. Everything that I put before the altar is the freshest and best we have. This long silver manger is where I put little candies. The children never take it—they know it's for the gods. Yes, every home in Mongolia keeps those peacock feathers—they purify the home.

*A quart jar is full of incense. Dewajao spoons some onto a small dish and lights it, then waves the smoke around her waist three times. The mixture smells as though it is mostly juniper.*

*The husband brings a lump of dried dung from the kitchen.* From a cow's behind! *he says vigorously.* We have electricity but this is our main fuel.

Water? We carry it in. We have water tickets to buy water. *He goes to get the tickets, allowing his wife to resume her story. It is difficult, often impossible, to talk to a woman without the husband taking over as the main focus of attention. Even questions addressed directly to the wife are still naturally answered by the husband.*

*Now that the husband has gone, she continues.* The *argal** is free for us. My children collect it. We don't have to buy it since we have our own cows, but other families have to buy. It isn't usually sold in Ulaanbaatar. In the countryside it costs between 40 and 100 tugriks for one package.

How do we buy water? Every family has to go to the Department Store in Ulaanbaatar to buy water tickets! We buy our tickets once every month and I pay around 2,000 tugriks for them [$4]. See these little squares? Each square is equivalent to forty liters of water. We take them to a small brick building around ten minute's walk away and the man inside fills our jar with water. A hose comes out of the window and there's a guard standing by. You can't just fill as much as you want.

Come on outside and see my vegetables. Here, I started growing these two years ago: cabbage, potatoes, and garlic. My children like them; they're not for me. They could eat up this little plot of vegetables in two days. But it helps, it means we don't have to buy so many.

This house is new. We built it three years ago. Before then we lived here in a ger, which I prefer. A ger is warmer, and better for old people. But we want to keep our ger for a long time, so we've folded it up and put it away. We have to take care of it.

That's the outhouse over there in the corner. How often do we empty it? well, that depends. Depends on the size of the hole mainly. If it's a big hole it lasts ten years, if a smaller hole only five years. That's a relatively new hole there.

So this is my life. I've lived in this spot now for seventeen years. Since my son was born. And I will be here till I die.

*She waves goodbye at the gate, gleaming ruddy cheeks and strong white teeth expressing as much warmth and hospitality as is possible.*

Come again, whenever you can!

*Cows in particular are often seen wandering around Ulaanbaatar.*

*Argal is the Mongolian word for dried cow dung.*

*In Mongolia, the sutras are generally written in the Tibetan script, although sometimes in Mongolian. Individual pages are stacked and then wrapped in a silk cloth, and kept on the altar as a form of offering.*

*Lamas blew a white conch shell in monasteries to call monks to prayer.*

*A thanka is a painting depicting Buddhist deities.*

*This is where Dewajao gets her water. The hose is connected to a tank inside the building. Small square coupons, bought at the Department Store in town, are handed to the man inside, behind the window.*

*page 57: Dewajao sitting in her one-room house. Her bed is behind on her left, her seven children sleep on the floor where she is sitting. A small shrine, enhanced by a large clock, is behind on her right.*

FACTURE JOB: *Oyuntsetseg*

*O*yuntsetseg lives in a one-room wooden building in the middle of a field on the edge of a small town called Ulaantolgoi.\* The road between Erdenet and Ulaanbaatar runs nearby.

*The sun is going down when we stop, and the temperature is dropping fast. We are in need of a place to spend the night. Husband and wife immediately invite us in, give us tea, and make us welcome, though this visit by strangers as night is falling is completely unexpected.*

*Their one-room home is warm and cozy. A wood stove soon has water boiling for tea. The stove is set in a sunken part of the floor, directly on the earth. Oyuntsetseg stays beside it throughout the evening, and also during our breakfast the next morning. She does not come to sit in the 'living room' area with her husband and guests.*

*She has a bandanna around her head, holding back long black hair. Her face glows with young, animated excitement.*

I was born here in this *somon.*\* My husband as well, so that both of our mothers are nearby and can help with the children. We're lucky. You see, I have a job at Erdenet, the big copper mine. I spend Monday through Thursday nights there, staying with my mother-in-law, then come back here to spend Friday night, Saturday and Sunday with my husband.

We've been married two years. We have two children. One is two years old and the other is four. My husband works in water control, as a technical assistant working with equipment.

*The husband is good looking, small boned but well built. The two of them make a handsome couple.*

I am 24; my husband is 25. We built this house ourselves. It's for the summer only—when winter comes, we'll put up the ger in the yard. A lot of people are building themselves wooden houses now and keeping the gers only for winter. Our neighbors across the way have their ger inside the house until the construction is done. That keeps them even more protected from the wind.

I still think of myelf as a country girl. Not a city girl. For example, I keep cows and chickens. Three cows, although only one gives milk. I get up at 5:30 in the morning to milk it; my mother does it for me when I'm not here. We also have a horse, but we want to sell it. *She glances at her husband.* We've had a little financial difficulty and need the money. What's the price? Well, we're charging 60,000 tugriks for it [$120]. That's not expensive. That's a normal price for a horse.

Water? I get my water from the somon center, up in the town. It has to be brought down by vehicle. I pay 50 *mongo** for every liter. If I could transport it myself it would be less. I'm paying more than half of the 50 mongo just for the transport.

We can't use the river water here, since it isn't fresh. It comes from Erdenet Lake, which has been polluted by the mine. Even with the water we buy, I have to strain it through this little sieve to get the larger particles out.

No, we didn't pay anything for our land here. We just put the house here and have been allowed to stay. If somebody came from some-where else and put up a house, I think there would be no problem. But it is probably easier if you are registered as a member of the somon. Nor do we pay any taxes. We haven't been asked to pay taxes.

We also have chickens. *She is proud of this, and doesn't let the subject of animals go without mentioning the chickens.* The dogs are chained near them, outside there, to guard them from animals.

We cut the wood we use for cooking from the forest, above the town.

*The house is extremely clean. Oyuntsetseg was not expecting visitors, but every article is dusted and in its place. The colors make it lively and inviting, and the warmth is welcome as winter winds gather force out-side. Old wooden chests decorate one end of the room. Two have Mongolian designs, one has a Russian motif and was passed down to the husband by a great-grandfather. Pillows are fluffed and neatly set on the bed. The embroidery on the pillowcases shows Mickey Mouse surrounded by peacocks.*

*We sleep in their yard, frost heavy on our tent in the morning. She makes us ganbir for breakfast, a kind of fried bread cooked like a pancake. She uses homemade butter for the oil and then breaks four eggs into the pan* to make fried eggs. We eat with our fingers, breaking off pieces. The milk tea is steaming hot and very welcome.

This family is one generation away from the steppe. They live in the same place all year and keep a few animals, but they also have steady jobs. The old customs, nonetheless, are as strong as ever. Oyuntsetseg's husband never takes a sip of airak without first flicking a little with his third finger to the spirits hovering around. He never hands or takes something from his wife or anyone else without touching his left hand to his right elbow as he does it. The hospitality of both is as strong as it ever was in the nomadic tradition.

Life is not easy, but the smiles of these two are radiant, their gladness at being able to share with us is apparent. Oyuntsetseg soon has to leave to collect her children. She keeps turning around to wave goodbye. There is a spring in her step and she is happy.

*The name Ulaantolgoi means 'Red Hill.'*

*A sum is the same as a somon, or county, an administrative unit in an aimag.*

*Tugriks are divided into mongo, one hundred mongo per tugrik.*

Oyuntsetseg bringing in the milk on a very cold morning.

POLITICS & LAW

OFFICE OF THE PRESIDENT: *Jama*

*Jama is generally known in Mongolia as 'Jama of the Office of the President.' She has been foreign policy advisor to President Ochirbat for the past five years and she is a well-known figure in Mongolia. The public knows her from her two years as news anchorwoman on the national television channel. The close-knit elite in Mongolia knows her as 'one of us.' Foreign aid organizations, whose money forms a significant part of the country's budget, know her as one of the few establishment figures considered to be progressive and a force for democratic reform.*

Mongolia has bought a car called democracy. But we have not yet been able to drive this car—we lack spare parts, but most importantly we lack fuel. The car stands in the garage, something for us to show people.

The fuel is the mentality. You see, Mongolia has never had such an animal as a 'citizen.' To the average person, government was something over there, beyond the next hill. Participation in government has been a foreign concept.

Ever since I was involved in translating Party documents, and certainly by the mid-1980s, I was aware of hints to the effect that Mongolia was receiving massive 'loans' from the Soviet Union. They would say, 'Capital investments in the national economy have been mustered with 70% foreign aid.' The word 'mustered' still amuses me.

Knowledgeable people said the 'investments' were more like 100%. Every couple of years the Russians would forgive the debt. Nobody cared. The government was glad to have this continue, for nobody imagined that the Soviet Union would collapse! Nobody seemed to mind that we were a captive nation.

*Jama has short-cropped hair and a bar-room toughness about her. She speaks English fluently, though Russian is her first language, then Mongolian, then French. Her accent is more European than American. She is a member of one of the three main parties in opposition to the ruling party in government.*

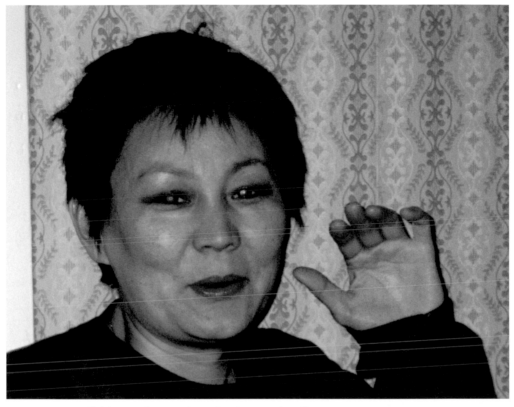

*Jama, astute politician and campaigner for democratic reform.*

What is the platform of our National Democratic Party? Take all the
nice words about democracy, plus a modicum of nationalistic coloring and you will have it. It's a conservative party, in one sense: family,
private property. We are rather tired of all this proletarian business.
So, yes, elitist.

At the same time, we are, I should say, very liberal. We put humans
above the State. The sun revolves around the human being. We stand
for human rights, for freedoms. And this, you must understand, is
very non-Asian. It conflicts with Asian traditions.

What makes this country different from other Asian countries is its
nomadic heritage. The State existed but never interfered much in
people's lives. Levels of personal freedom here and in the United States
are very comparable.

But the last five years have been a period of self-identification. Now with the pullout of Soviet assistance we are in a new situation. To outsiders, we have seemed so unfortunate, such a hapless nation: three hundred years under the Manchus, seventy years under Russia. But in fact life was easy, being protected by others made us complacent. As a result, we lost our identity. We unlearned how to take care of ourselves. Mongolia was allowed to sleep.

*Until 1990, Mongolia survived and thrived on aid from the Soviet Union. With the dissolution of the USSR, the country experienced a fairly smooth and bloodless change of government.*

Briefly, here's what happened. In March of 1990, the Politburo of the former Communist Party stepped down because of a hunger strike. The General Secretary of the Party stepped down too. Since he had simultaneously been Head of State, the Great People's Hural, our Parliament, had to find a new President. They selected a young and dynamic man who had been Minister of Foreign Trade, named Ochirbat.

Then, in June '93, we held direct Presidential elections. Ochirbat was re-elected by direct popular vote. At that point, his old Party decided to dump him since he was beginning to disagree with their platform. Their policies were obsolete and they were incapable of any new initiatives, any real governing. Ochirbat was adopted by the opposition parties as their own candidate.

Meanwhile, in the Parliamentary elections of 1992, the liberal parties were voted out and a majority of old Communist Party members were voted back in. Yes, it is fair to say that the liberal parties were shocked by their losses in 1992. This was the result, however, of a classic case of gerrymandering. Proportional representation was redefined to give more weight to rural areas. Rural areas are conservative, so naturally the opposition lost.

Our party, as well as others, was then marginalized, psychologically and practically. We had to regroup, organize a new team, particularly at the level of advisors. It has been, I have to say, a failure. We have no stock reserve of experienced administrators. We have very limited human resources in Mongolia, not enough for real action.

*The next parliamentary elections are in June, 1996; the presidential election is in 1997. Not wanting to wait for elections before taking action, Jama recently helped draft a law on non-governmental organizations.*

Voluntary associations are, after all, the infrastructure of democracy, which otherwise is confined to occasional elections. A government cannot just do as it pleases with such organizations. Our government is so closed, so non-transparent, so corrupt—it will take empowered citizenry, people who are involved, to change it.

*Few people are as able as Jama to effect that change. She comes to her position with a background in politics and foreign affairs. Her family name is Sukhbaatar—the same name as the national hero whose statue stands in the center of Ulaanbaatar's main square. Her father was an Ambassador and Foreign Minister for many years.*

Has the name Sukhbaatar helped me? Of course. The family name gave me immunity during the old system, and it helps me now too. Our society is very small—as we say, there is 'no use hiding it and no use stating it.'

*Despite this association with the old guard, Jama is known as a rebel.*

How do I spend my time these days? Being sad—no, being angry, at this government of ours. Isn't it ironic that it is the Mongolian Communists who have benefited most from Mongolia's nascent capitalism. This would bother me less if it were the young ones, who are starting out. But it is the same people who for seventy years were fooling their own people. Now they are simply becoming common thieves.

*For the time being, Jama says she is not interested in holding office. One hopes this may change.*

*Natural History Museum. This building houses the famous dinosaurs from the Gobi. The Museum is a two-minute walk north from Sukhbaatar Square. Until recently, public sculpture has been a feature of Ulaanbaatar. A large statue of Stalin was removed in the early 1990s from its position in front of the Public Library, and Stalin now lies on his back in a crate behind the Library. Statues of Choibalsan still dot the city, and Lenin still strides in front of the Ulaanbaatar Hotel. Much of the sculpture is apolitical or relates to Mongolian culture; little new sculpture is being commissioned.*

*Statue of Sukhbaatar, National Hero, in Sukhbaatar Square.*

CONSTITUTIONAL COURT: *Sarantuya*

*Government House extends across the northern side of Sukhbaatar Square, which is in the middle of Ulaanbaatar. The building looks like a smaller version of the Great Hall of the People in China. Immediately in front of it is a small mausoleum, where the remains of Choibalsan and Sukhbaatar are said to be kept.*

*Entry into Government House is not easy. Public access is forbidden. The entire right wing of the building was formerly the headquarters of the Communist Party; after 1990, the Party was ousted and set up its offices in a small building nearby. The rooms of the eastern wing are now used by various government offices, including the office of the Constitutional Court.*

Welcome. This is my office and the office of the Constitutional Court of Mongolia. The roses came from one of the few greenhouses in Ulaanbaatar. I'm glad to have been able to find them for your visit; in March, it is not easy to have fresh flowers!

Mongolia's constitution was passed in 1992, before the change in government. A working group of eight people drafted it. I was one of the eight. My contribution related specifically to the structure of the state.

I am glad to say that international observers consider Mongolia's constitution to be one of the best in the world. For a start, it is realistic. It does not represent a radical departure from the previous legal system. Mongolian laws were already fairly consistent with traditional continental law, so the new constitution did not change the entire system. Germany is the classic example of continental law, and Mongolia's constitution reflects German influence.

Naturally there are special features of Mongolia that required appropriate changes. Mongolia is a small country, with different systems and a different culture. Together with the Constitution, the country established a Constitutional Court. This was something new. Mongolia had never had such a thing before. It was established under the Constitution as a permanent body, not an interim institution dependent on the governing party.

*Sarantuya: a lawyer and a member of the committee that drafted Mongolia's new constitution. International observers consider it to be one of the finer constitutions in the world.*

This independence makes it unusual. There is an ongoing debate about the status of this Court. Mongolia has three branches of power, legislative, executive, and judiciary. The judiciary branch consists of both the Ministry of Justice and the Constitutional Court.

Some people say, for instance, that the Ministry of Justice is not truly independent but more a tool of the Government. I don't want to comment on that. By mandate of the Constitution, this Court at least is a separate, independent institution. Some of my friends call it a mainstay against totalitarianism.

Am I hopeful about the future of this country? There are a number of transformations occurring in Mongolia right now. I am concerned that the outcome include a proper structure for political and democratic processes. What we do should benefit people in concrete ways. The purpose of our work is to give a decent life to regular people, not just a lot of talk about freedom and democracy.

The problems are extreme right now. People are experiencing uncertainty and trauma as the situation changes. Economic reform is coming along well. Unfortunately, legal reform is one of the last areas to be considered in Mongolia. As a lecturer at the University, I try to provide students with objective information. In general I support democratic initiatives; when it comes to supporting a particular party, I abstain. I would rather evaluate the structure in which the parties operate.

My position on the parliamentary elections in 1996 and the presidential elections in 1997 is this: I will abide by the law and not be driven by any party or by any special interest. My aim is to assure that there is a proper legal structure, within which concerns can be addressed by all sides.

*Sarantuya's manner is very firm and very calm. One does not expect such self-contained strength from a lady who wears fluffy lace at the neck. The pin on her lapel is tasteful, the frames of her glasses are sophisticated. Her makeup is perfect and her black suit is immaculate.*

Women lawyers? There are many in Mongolia, but most are criminal lawyers. In addition, over half of Mongolian judges are women. Very few women, however, have gone into constitutional law. My father was a criminal lawyer and as a result I was familiar with the concepts

*Government House. The wing on the right is where the offices of the Constitutional Court are located.*
*The small square structure in the middle houses the remains of Choibalsan, former head of government.*

*right: The opera house on Sukhbaatar Square.*

*below: A typical street in the center of Ulaanbaatar, near Government House. Concrete apartment blocks have been built around the perimeter of the city, but the central area retains a certain charm.*

of a legal system from childhood. In school there were, as you may know, quotas for different subjects. Too many people opted for criminal law, so I chose constitutional law. Of course, no-one knew at the time that the entire situation in Mongolia would change.

I studied first in Russia. I went there at the age of seventeen, then on to the GDR, East Germany, when I was twenty. I did my doctorate in jurisprudence in East Germany: the degree was actually in Public Law, with a concentration in Constitutional Law.

In addition to serving as Advisor to the Constitutional Court, I also teach at the University. I consider this to be extremely important. The legal field in Mongolia is obsolete. I would greatly appreciate communicating with law schools and law firms in the United States. My students need exposure and western training. I have some ties to Germany but to date no ties at all in the United States. Anyone can write to me about this; a letter to Sarantuya, Government House, Constitutional Court, Ulaanbaatar, Mongolia will reach me.

No, I am not one of the nine members of the Constitutional Court. There is a restriction on age: members must be at least 40 years old. I am 35.

AT HOME: *Dash*

*D*ash lives in a gutted building on the outskirts of Ulaanbaatar. The six-story cement block was built by the Chinese in 1953. The central part of the roof has collapsed and the heating system for the building has broken down.*

*To get there, you walk down a path between fences. People are growing vegetables in plots just visible between the tall boards. This used to be a Chinese district. The Chinese left in the mid-1970s, when Tsedenbal's policy changed and thousands were summarily sent home. A number of Inner Mongolian Chinese have recently begun to come back to Mongolia.*

We moved here in 1974. It was fine then. We had heat and we had running water. When the Chinese left, I began work in the greenhouse nearby. Since it was for the government, I had a regular salary.

*We sit facing each other on the two beds in the room. The room also holds a table, and a chest with two TVs on top of it. Nothing more. The newer television set is sitting on top of a very old one. There is a rug on one wall for warmth, but no other decoration in the room. Dash has lived in this room for 21 years.*

I have eight children, five boys and three girls. Three of my children go to school, sometimes. The others are unemployed.

*She sits very still, one hand over the other. A scarf covers her head. She is aware of her poverty and looks cowed and broken.* My eldest children sell little things on the street. We try to eat every day. We have no cows, or sheep, or land. We just live here.

I do have a pension now. But it is 3,750 tugriks per month—not enough to buy food. My husband's pension is 5,352 tugriks per month. This is also not enough [a total of $18 per month between them]. So we eat the same thing every day: bread and tea.

*A bowl of bread has been placed out for my visit. The bread is cut in chunks. She is not able to offer milk with the tea.*

When I worked in the greenhouse, raising vegetables, the salary was low, so now my pension is low. The greenhouse was associated with this building. People who worked there were assigned to live here.

There's no running water. I carry it in from outside. There is a well to the west of the building. *She nods vigorously as she describes this. She wants to tell someone what she does every day, how she lives.* Every twenty liters of water cost me 16 tugriks. I sometimes use 80 liters a day, sometimes 120 liters. I carry it up the stairs. No, the toilet is broken—we use one outside.

There's also no heat. There used to be. *She indicates the hot-water radiator on the wall.* But it broke over two years ago.

*The walls are painted in Chinese fashion, green on the bottom half, white on top. There is electricity, as evidenced by one bare lightbulb hanging from the ceiling. High ceilings make the room more spacious but also more cold—something to consider when temperatures go down to 40 degrees below zero.*

I get up at about eight every morning. But then I have nothing to do. No sewing, nothing. I sit here at home. Sometimes I go into Ulaanbaatar—just to look.

I don't know anything about politics or laws, but our life is difficult. It was better before than it is now, but I think the future will be better. I believe in 'better'...

After the heating broke, in the last couple of years it has been very bad. *She is barely audible as she says,* I'm not sure what I am going to do this winter.

*page 79: Dash, sitting on her bed, with a rug on the wall behind for warmth. Her building is unheated. Unlike in a ger, there is no stove for burning wood and dung. Unheated buildings are not uncommon in Ulaanbaatar.*

*The building in which Dash and her family live.*

## BUDDHISM & TRADITION

### PAINTER OF MONGOL ZURAG: *Baatar*

*Baatar is a buxom, stylish, modern woman. We meet in her apartment, near central Ulaanbaatar. Her husband and daughter are also present. Her soft and feminine manner does not hide the fact that she is a serious and committed artist.*

I am a professional painter. My paintings are in the style of Mongol Zurag, a traditional and native style of Mongolian painting. *Zurag* means 'picture' or 'painting' in Mongolian.

Mongol Zurag is different from thanka painting in many ways. Thanka painters followed a canon. There were rules about what and how to paint that related to subject, colors, and proportions: most of a given painting was strictly controlled. Thankas were official paintings, the expression of the ruling religious authorities. Mongol Zurag, on the other hand, have always been simple and free.

Of course, Mongol Zurag painting was constrained by the Russians here. Until quite recently, we were tightly controlled in what we were allowed to say or paint. For instance, we were not allowed to paint or portray Chinggis Khan, or even to talk about him. To the Russians, he was a killer. He killed many Russians in particular. So that subject, as well as others relating to Mongolian legends, was forbidden to us.

Perhaps it is due to this recent control that I now focus exclusively on traditional Mongolian subjects. I paint the old legends and the history, particularly the folk history, of our country.

Why not paint these subjects in a modern style? First, because the modern school of painting in Mongolia uses different techniques. If I switched to modern styles, I would lose my hand. Traditional Mongol Zurag requires techniques that are not used in contemporary painting. For the past seventy years, Mongolia has faced towards the West. In fact, we feel rather more western than oriental, and our painting has reflected this. Many of our painters were trained in Moscow, St. Petersburg, Prague.

Secondly, one can already see in Mongol Zurag elements of modernism, as well as tradition. If one is trained in modern art, one sees in these paintings certain aspects that European painters were experimenting with earlier in this century. The use of color is one example, and the use of space on the canvas is another. It may appear 'primitive,' but in fact the painter uses a carefully controlled palette of hues to express the mood and emotion of a given painting. The use of space on the canvas is also controlled and composed, to show rhythm and emotion. Composition is as important in Mongol Zurag as it is in a European painting.

But most importantly, perhaps, the subject matter lends itself to this style of painting, this Mongol Zurag. The point is to make a painting evocative, to show emotion and joy, not just to depict something.

The subjects of thanka paintings were inevitably the gods. In contrast, Mongol Zurag are more direct: they are about the people, the animals, and the life of Mongolians. Mongol Zurag allows a painter to illustrate the whole experience of living as a Mongolian.

Take this painting, for example. It tells the legend of the origins of the Mongolian people, how they descended from a wolf and a deer. The opening lines of the *Secret History of the Mongols* say, "There was a bluish wolf, born with a destiny from Heaven above. His spouse was a fallow doe...." From these two came the ancestors of Chinggis Khan.

This ancient legend pervades the Mongolian culture. One could not portray it before, but it is in our blood.

Yes, naturally there are horses in this painting too. The horse is present as a matter of course. Mongolians and horses are inseparable. One cannot think of one without the other.

This next painting shows the process of catching and taming horses. Our horses are half-wild, since they spend the winter on the steppe without herding or attention. This painting shows how a yearling is caught in the spring with a long pole and rope; then a man, a very strong man, gets on him to start training. First without a bridle, since the horse won't stand for a bridle. Then, in this section, the horses ears are held as the first bridle is put on. The whole process is shown in a continuum in the same painting.

A Mongol Zurag painting shows everything up front. Nothing is hidden or esoteric. Here is life as it is. In this painting of the inside of a ger, for instance, you see the mother suckling her child, you see men drinking *shimiin arkhi,** you see the baby animals that are kept inside with the family, since it's cold outside. The ger is hot. You see the flames of the fire and the smoke. This is exactly how it is in the countryside today.

The upfrontness of a painting does not mean random placement. Each group is composed to lead the eye to other groups, while colors and rhythms are carefully considered  to make the whole painting a single unit. Again, I believe European painters in the early twentieth century experimented with these matters: simultaneous presentation, juxtaposition of dream states, and emotions and customs.

I was raised in Gobi Altai aimag, which has many camels. Since I grew up with them, I paint camels a lot. Here are two camel stallions fighting. Camels do fight in the winter, especially, with the sand swirling around and the fur flying.

How do I know how to paint Chinggis Khan? I study all the historical references I can find. Most portraits use the famous Chinese painting as their primary reference; this painting is now in the Palace Museum in Taipei. Unfortunately, it's inaccurate in a number of ways that we can identify. He did not wear an earring in his right ear, for example, and his hair was pulled up in back, not down as in that portrayal. The first Mongolian painter that we know of who portrayed Chinggis Khan, a man named Horgoson Horch, painted his portrait in around 1230. He was a Mongolian painter, but he worked in China in an official capacity.

We were allowed to read the *Secret History of the Mongols* in school, but that was the extent of our knowledge about Chinggis Khan. We had no sense of him as a king, as a man who united Mongolians into one powerful country. There has been a movement by historians to learn more about this period, and I talk to them about the visual details in order to paint my historical works.

I also use a lot of traditional motifs in my paintings, which represent the visual vocabulary of the old Mongolia. Interlocking circles, for example, refer to a married man, while interlocking triangles refer to a married woman. Many women wear a ring with interlocking triangles on it, which means they are married. Some of the symbolism comes from the thanka tradition, but of course the origins of many symbols date from long before Buddhism came to Mongolia.

I do perhaps thirty paintings a year. Right now, I also go to school. After graduating from the Art Institute I painted for many years, but now I feel the need and also have the opportunity to learn more. One can now find out about things that were formerly prohibited. I will be learning about *tsam,* for instance, the ritual dance and prayer drama of Mongolia. It incorporates ancient shamanist elements. This tradition, and the study of it, was forbidden until the late 1980s.

Before 1990 I worked professionally as a painter for the government. I would take commissions and paint what was required. Since the change of government, I have painted on my own, here at home as well as in a small studio I have. There is no salary. I get along by selling paintings. Several of us share a gallery; we rent the space together. A number of my paintings are now in Germany and Japan, some also in France.

Very few painters are doing authentic traditional painting now. There are perhaps two or three. Many students graduate from the Art Institute every year, but most paint in the European style. Only a few of us are concerned about maintaining the traditions.

*\*Shimiin arkhi is home-brewed vodka made from cow's milk. It is distilled, whereas airak, made from mare's milk, is fermented.*

*Baatar is painting Mongol Zurag, a native form of folk painting. Symbolic elements here include the metal-banded hearth, placed over the fire, on top of which the daily meal was cooked.*

*The Art Museum in Ulaanbaatar. This museum houses some well-known nineteenth-century Mongol Zurag paintings, such as those attributed to B. Sharav that describe traditional Mongolian life. It also houses the famous gilded bronze sculptures by Zanabazar (seventeenth century), as well as many thankas. It is one of three main repositories of traditional Mongolian art in Ulaanbaatar.*

*Gandan Monastery in Ulaanbaatar. This building is the center of Buddhism in the country, and is a working monastery with a school as well as prayer hall.*

BUDDHIST: *Puntsag Dulam*

*Puntsag Dulam lives in Hovsgol aimag, in northwestern Mongolia. Her home is a tiny kitchen adjoining her son's small wooden house in the town of Moron. The room contains a wood stove with stools around it, and a bed.*

*She sits on the bed, in a lavender del with green buttons. This more formal attire has just been put on for the occasion. She will not allow a photograph without first changing into her best del.*

*She also refuses to smile for the camera. Lack of teeth may be one reason (she has one tooth, in front), but the tradition is also to look solemn in a photograph. She sits with great composure, pulling her hem demurely over her knees. Immediately after the shutter clicks, she beams broadly and radiates good cheer.*

I am 70 years old.

Yes, and I am a Buddhist. My son says I am a 'good' Buddhist. I don't know. It led to problems earlier.

*The walls of her little kitchen are lined with photographs of the Dalai Lama. There are tsam\* posters and also an altar that faces the door.*

Those two parcels wrapped in silk on the altar are sutras. The silk wrapping for a sutra is also called a del, a sutra del. Making dels for sutras is one of the virtuous acts, like copying the sutras themselves. I can't read the words. They were passed down to me by my grandparents. But having them there is 'good.'

How do I feel when foreigners come here? I feel I want to give of myself to people. When they come here, I am glad. I feel I am not empty. Inside me, *she indicates great capacity,* I am big, not small.

*She is cutting up pure mutton fat, for her son's dinner.* We want to give ourselves. That's how I feel.

*How do you feel about the change in government?*

I feel that this must be. We *must* change. It was impossible to live the same, to continue as we were.

*Puntsag Dulam in her best lavender and green del. Puntsag Dulam's house is small, but not her outlook on the world.*

In the villages, where there are no schools, there is no information. We need a flow of knowledge. Here in Moron, it's better. There are more teachers. In some villages there is not even a radio. One needs to be situated where there is access to information.

*Behind her is a poster advertising an exhibition of French clocks. It comes from the Pavlovsk Palace Museum and looks incongruous behind this old woman in a lavender del, sitting in a shack. But Puntsag Dulam has a range of concerns far beyond her kitchen and her own person.*

*Does she go to the new hiid?\* (There is a newly reconstructed temple in town—the old one was destroyed.)*

*A long pause....*You can't take one thing and just place it inside another so easily.

*Earlier, out in the street, she admired the brooms being sold by an itinerant peddler, one of which is now given to her. The broom is nothing but a sheaf of wheat stalks tied together around a stick, but her joy at receiving it is boundless.*

*Her kitchen is a tiny haven of warmth and hospitality. Her son's room, next door, is only slightly more roomy. The bristly back of a hedgehog is tied over his door for good luck.*

*The two live here alone. The father died in 1989. A daughter works in Erdenet, the big copper-mine town. The children take turns when they can, looking after this gracious and generous mother.*

*\*A hiid is a Buddhist temple.*

*\*Tsam is the ritual exorcist dance-and-prayer drama of Mongolia, incorporating both Buddhist and shamanist elements.*

*Puntsag Dulam's daughter, Altantsetseg, tending the stove.*

NEAR A COALMINE: *Oyuna*

*T*his woman was reluctant to let us in. She looked us over as she talked for a while to our driver. There was no instant hospitality here. She was cautious and at first unfriendly. We had run out of gas and had to endure the cold. We were ready for a hot cup of tea in a friendly ger. Finally, when she saw her husband approaching, she agreed to allow us inside.

*By the time we were settled and had explained our predicament, her manner had changed. The initial caution of a person who lives in proximity to crime, however, was similar to what one might encounter in a large city. 'Civilization' in the form of the nearby coalmine had encroached on the idyll.*

It's getting cold out there! Too cold to cook your lunch over a fire in the open. Please use my stove. I'm sorry about the dog. He has to be held back when strangers are around.

Yes, it's warm inside here. Sit there in the sun. Never mind, you can sit in the north, no need to be formal. A ger is a natural sundial.* You can see there are eighty-eight rods radiating from the center to the side walls. We know exactly what time it is by how the sun, coming through that open central hole, hits the rods. Since the sun hits straight to the north, it's time for lunch!

*She used dried cow dung for the fire and soon had tea boiling.*

This is the basket we use to collect argal. You know there are many different kinds of dung, and each has a different name; argal is only used for cow droppings, not the others. Horse droppings are second best, sheep droppings are used only if necessary. Cow droppings are best, of course, since they burn hotter and longer.

My children, and also my husband and I, collect argal every day. You must have seen the coal mine near here. It is probably the biggest in Mongolia. The coal is just like a huge black ocean beneath us. So we also use coal here in addition to argal.

*After lunch (we cooked our own food on the family's stove) we hear about this family's wealth in livestock. The increase in herd numbers is*

*becoming an environmental problem in Mongolia. The cashmere goat population in particular has increased dramatically, leading to overgrazing of certain areas and a sharp drop in the quality of cashmere. This is also bringing down the price of cashmere but, to most people, large flocks still represent wealth.*

My husband and I are fortunate to have a number of animals: several hundred. My children help tend them. Some people find this a 'sad' place, with the mine and all the lorries carrying the coal, but it's good for us. We're not city people but we're near communications and transport. That's good for my children.

That little bag? We hang that from the center of the ger every time we put it up. It's to keep the home safe and well. Inside are herbs. No, it's not Buddhist, it's just tradition.

That is the family altar. My husband has many sutras, written in Sanskrit and Tibetan. He comes from Inner Mongolia. How many years has he been here? Around two hundred years. That is to say, his tribe was originally from Inner Mongolia.

Each family has its own god. Also each individual. The god protects them, so they keep secret who it is. If someone knew, he would know which god to say charms against. As a result, we often keep the god covered up, whether it is a statue or a painting. We have to be careful.

Mongolia is changing, but I suppose we do keep the old traditions. It's just normal life. We don't even think about it.

*\*The sun comes through the opening in the top of the ger. A square piece of felt is used to cover this opening when it is stormy; one corner of the felt is pulled back on clear days and the opening lets in air and sunshine.*

*Open-pit coalmine at Bayanteeg.*

*page 95: A typical Mongolian stove. The flue goes up and out the opening in the top of the ger; wood, dung or coal is inserted in the front.*

*above: The rope dangling from the center of the ger is tucked under the struts in this manner. Easy, quick retrieval is the functional reason; the shape is made in the form of a wolf's snout, to scare away evil.*

*left: This bag hanging from the top of the ger contains a mixture of grasses and herbs, and is put up for the health and prosperity of the family.*

*The top opening of a ger creates a natural sundial inside the room. As the sun traverses the sky, it passes over the rods of the ger, one by one, in the opposite direction.*

*The husband demonstrates here how he uses fork and basket to collect dried dung from the steppe to use as fuel in the stove.*

## GOBI LANDSCAPE

### WOMAN WHOSE FATHER IS BEATING WOOL FOR FELT

*We were travelling crosscountry in the south-eastern part of the Gobi Altai.\* Our jeep had been bucking up and down over ravine after ravine; shadows were getting longer and we were not making noticeable progress. We finally admitted to ourselves that we were lost.*

*We had not seen anyone for hours. Finally we came across a young boy on his horse tending sheep. He didn't know where we wanted to go, but pointed in the direction of his family ger. This turned out to be only a few minutes' drive away.*

*She was standing on the hillside, across a small gully from three gers that formed the family commune. When we beckoned, she strode across with vigor and pleasure—an open and friendly expression on an intelligent face. This was not one of the destitute women one meets in the Gobi, with five children by five different fathers and no man to help provide, impoverished in spirit as well as material means.*

Hello! Yes, we know the way to Tsagaan Agui. It's further to the north there, on the southern slope of those far mountains. You've been going in the wrong direction.

How do we know? We don't really know exactly—we've never been to Tsagaan Agui. But we have heard there is a cave to the north that has been lived in by very ancient peoples. We don't herd our animals that far north ourselves. We stay in this area, between Ikh Bogd and Baga Bogd.\*

Here *(looking at our map, from the Andrews expedition of 1925),* this is where we are now. This is where you want to go.

These are our gers. Our family lives together in one group—my father is in the back there, beating felt. You want to see felt being made? Come. This is called a 'one-more ger'—it's a small one, kept just for storing things. Here's my father, beating the wool fibers with these two metal rods. Then we wet it and roll it with the horse pulling and so on. But that comes later.

*The grandmother of this clan (third from left, in felt boots) is eighty-four. Her daughter stands next to her. A horse, seen in the background, is invariably tethered near a ger, saddled and ready for action should the need arise.*

No, the land is not as poor as it looks. We get by here. Have you seen the gazelles? We have thousands of gazelles around us. You may see them going up to Tsagaan Agui. They're like a rolling river passing over the landscape. Yes, we're doing fine. We have enough.

*\*The Gobi Altai are mountain ranges that run like fingers from the west into the central Gobi. They are dry, precipitous, and inhospitable; among other wild animals, they harbor snow leopards.*

*\* Ikh means great or big, Baga means small. These are two mountains with their subsidiary ranges in the Gobi Altai. They rise abruptly from the Gobi to over 3,800 meters, 12,000 feet.*

*Beating wool to make felt. The action separates and remixes the fibers, prior to rolling out, wetting, and then compressing. The compressing and drying make the fibers lock together.*

*A view of the landscape looking south from Tsagaan Agui towards this family's herding territory.*

WOMAN PUTTING UP GER

*From the ravines between the Ikh and Baga Bogd, we drove north until we hit the easternmost spur of the Ikh Bogd mountain range. We filled our water containers at a fortuitous well before heading for the deepest cleft in the hills that we could see on the skyline. The wells in the Gobi have been marked on maps for years; some of them are reinforced with Russian-built concrete structures. To start the water moving, you push the very long metal arm of a round central pump, walking in a circle until you hear splashing in the trough.*

*The mountains ahead of us had a feeling of great antiquity. Hunch-backed, treeless, seemingly plantless, they looked inhospitable. We pulled up to the gully leading to Tsagaan Agui as dark set in, pitched our tents in the sandy gully and went to sleep.*

*The next morning, before the first sun came across the wide valley to our south, we were up and ready to explore the cave. Tsagaan Agui means 'White Cave'; it is the earliest archaeological site yet found in Mongolia. By various dating methods, scientists estimate that the 'cultural layer,' the evidence of habitation, goes back at least 750,000 years. The site was deserted. A few camels grazed in the distance.*

*Later in the day we visited a family we had passed on the way into Tsagaan Agui. The day was clear and sunny and extremely cold. The family was taking advantage of the sunshine to declare this an 'auspicious day,' and to move its ger for the winter.*

Go ahead and take photographs! This is how we do it. I hold the center posts while he puts in the poles. Altogether 88 poles, although some gers use 108. He puts up a few on different sides and then I don't have to keep holding like this.

The door goes in that frame. First we put the eight sides up, those latticework panels, and run that horsehair rope around it to hold the panels in tight. Then we put the felt mats over the panels. Another couple of horsehair ropes will go around after the felt walls have been placed. We should be finished in an hour. As you can see, we're just moving from up there on the hill to down here, where the wind doesn't blow so hard.

Up there, we can see in all four directions. But it really is too windy. This is a *chartok.* When a storm comes through we tie a very large stone to this rope and hang it straight down. It keeps a gust from blowing the ger over. Oh yes, there are extremely strong winds here. The ger could easily be lifted off the ground. But those winds aren't usual, so we have the rope tucked under the poles most of the time.

Every part of putting up a ger has to be done just so. There's a reason for each move. Everything has its place, and there is a reason for the place. That makes it easy. As you can see from the cave, we Mongolians have lived here for a long time.

*previous page: Tsagaan Agui*

*below: With the sides of the ger removed, its furniture is left in a circle on the gound.*

carrying the felt sides
to the new location

holding up the two
central posts

inserting the roof
supports

WOMAN HERDER NEAR OROK NUR

*O*rok Nur* is in the distance—a shimmer of white salt rimming a deep blue body of water. A large ovoo, or ritual pile of stones, stands on a high point to the east of the lake. A woman sits on the ovoo, quietly looking out over the landscape. Her horse stands patiently, not attempting to eat the tough plants that grow up through the sandy soil. Soon she remounts and returns to the herd of sheep and goats, to lead them somewhere else to graze.

*Orok Nur was visited by the Andrews expedition in 1925. The old lakebed forms a flat expanse much greater than the current body of water. To the south, the mountains of the Ikh Bogd rise to a height of over 3,800 meters. This is one of the highest mountains in the country, lifting out of flat barren gobi. Quantities of paleolithic and neolithic stone tools have been washed down the steep slopes. Geodes and crystals are spread over the land. From the vantage point of the ovoo one can see for miles in every direction. There is not a person or a dwelling in sight.*

*A fox bounds out of a hiding place as we drive to the north. Around a dune, we come across the woman again, herding her flock. She smiles at us. Self-contained, not very curious about us, she seems a natural part of the violently beautiful landscape.*

*Nur means lake in Mongolian.*

*Orok Nur is in the distance; Ikh Bogd looms beyond the foothills to the left.*

### SINGLE WOMAN IN THE GOBI

*We had camped in a ravine about half a mile from her ger. The wind howled, the rain alternated with sleet, and we worried about a flash flood as we tried to sleep. In the morning, we heard a shout from across the way, a call to come visit.*

*Her home was not clean. Though her smile was broad, little cordiality accompanied the invitation to tea; this was a calculated move. We offered the lift in our jeep that she wanted, to visit relatives 'not far away.'*

*Yes, she had a husband, but he was a truck driver and often gone. Later she said her husband was out herding. A child rolled on the floor, vigorously scowling at us despite the pink chiffon ribbons in its hair. The child turned out to be a little boy dressed as a girl, his long hair pulled back in two ewer, or goat horns. The style is used to trick bad spirits into thinking a boy is a worthless girl, so that they will leave the child alone.*

I've been living here for four years. We came from further south in the Gobi. It took five days. We came by camel caravan, my brother-in-law, my sister, my family. The land was not as good down there, and we knew about this place. Nobody had settled here, so we moved in.

*In most parts of the country there is no apparent restriction on occupying unused land. Squatters' rights appear to prevail. International consultants are busily debating land-use laws for Mongolia. Meanwhile, the structures and restrictions of the previous Soviet regime have gone and people are moving, positioning themselves for the future.*

*We had camped in a sandy ravine in order to avoid the sharp rocks of an ancient lava flow that covered the ground. Yet these rocky slopes were considered fertile compared to her previous home.*

*Had she seen any wildlife in this rugged terrain?*

We saw a snow leopard a couple of years ago. It came down to the ger, right up to the door, and took some cheese.

*Did you actually see it?*

No, but later I saw the skin. My brother-in-law got it. It hadn't eaten any livestock. We just wanted the skin.

*The 'scowler' and his mother. With his hat on, this little 'girl' looks more like a little boy.*

*Her eyes were glazed from habitual drinking. Her skin was red and chapped. Surviving in a lava-field was not an easy life. Perhaps a previous man or a husband had once held a job. Now she relied on family to see her through.*

*She washed the child's hair by wetting it and slicking it back against his head, then pulled it again into two tight goat-horns. She dressed him, then started dressing herself. First she wound cotton cloth around her bare feet and stuck them in boots. A purple nylon blouse was put on over her cotton blouse. Over that went a simple del. Finally she tied a bright orange-and-purple scarf around her head. It wasn't enough clothing for the weather, but she said she was ready to go.*

*The stove was left to burn itself out. She ushered us through the door and then carefully locked it with a large padlock. It is not true that nobody locks his door to strangers in the Gobi.*

*Our first stop was her sister's ger, some ten minutes' drive to the south. There she picked up a bag full of 'goat,' the fur of which looked very much like fox. The decline in wild animals over the past five years in Mongolia has been precipitous, as people scour the land for any resources from which to earn a living. The sister's ger was above a ravine, looking out over miles of territory, spectacular but brutally inhospitable.*

*We drove miles back toward the north to another ger, flanked by two bronze-age tombs. Any place that is currently occupied by a ger in this region is almost sure to have large bronze-age mounds nearby. The criteria for selecting sites is the same now as it was then. Here the son was finally left behind in the grips of three grubby, older children. This was a terrifying prospect and he began to howl.*

*On we drove, to yet a third ger, this time around one hour to the north. There we left her, wishing her well and glad she was with family.*

*This is the family ger shown from the back. On the right is a stone shelter for animals. Two bronze-age graves stand to the right and left, outside the photo. Animals, humans, and graves are often found in the same protected and auspicious spots in the landscape.*

CAMELHERDER: *Dariimaa*

*Dariimaa lives in Gurvan Saikhan sum, in Middle Gobi aimag. Her family is prosperous: she and her husband and sons tend around two hundred sheep and goats and around sixty camels. Half are state-owned and the family gets the equivalent of a salary for looking after them. The other half are privately owned by the family.*

Camels are extremely noble animals. We Mongolians consider them to be kind, patient, and generous.

There is a folktale about camels that tells how the mighty camel lost his magnificent set of antlers. He went down to the spring one day to drink, and there he met a deer who had been coveting his antlers. The deer asked if he could borrow them, just for one day. The camel, thinking that one day could not hurt, said yes. Next day, the camel went to the spring to retrieve his antlers, but the deer wasn't there. To this day, the camel will drink, then look out over the landscape, trying to see that deer. But the deer will never come. We use the word *genin* to describe the camel. It means someone who is overly generous, to his own detriment. This story about *genin* is something every child knows.

The camels are sheared in June. It takes around three days, and everyone helps. Some people comb the hair out but we just shear the animals. We get nearly all the products we need from camels: camel's milk to drink, meat to eat, fibers for clothes. We use camel dung for fuel, both in winter and summer.

*above: Camel's dung, the primary fuel for this camelherding family. Camel dung is called 'horgol' in Mongolian. It is collected all summer, for use in the bitterly cold Gobi winters.*

*left: The wooden barrel into which fresh camel's milk is poured every day, called a 'hohuur.' The plunger on top helps stir the gently fermenting mixture. The milk is extremely rich and nutritious; the taste is slightly tangy.*

*right: The small bag above the ceremonial cloth, which is blue, contains earth from the spot where Dariimaa and her husband Sukh were married. This small bag accompanies the family whenever they move, which is three or four times a year.*

*This baby camel is one of ten new camels born this year in Darimaa's herd. Newly born camels are called 'torom,' yearlings are called 'botgo.' Darimaa has had a total of twenty-four torom and botgo in the last two years. Baby camels are born in March and April. Unlike goats, they are not usually brought into the ger to be hand-fed. This little camel has a bright pink patch of fabric on its nose halter, to identify it. Babies are kept tied to a long rope on the ground as their mothers are being milked.*

*Two of Darimaa's herd of around sixty camels. These Bactrian camels live to be fourteen or fifteen years old; they can be ridden from the age of five or six, and a good strong one, like the camel at the right, is in his prime at the age of seven. The saddle for a camel is made without any wood, unlike the saddles used on horses. The carpet underneath is called a 'tohom,' the thicker, shaped carpet on top is called a 'toksh.' Camel stirrups are also very different from the stirrups Mongolians use on horse saddles. Horse-saddle stirrups are nearly round and heavy, since the rider stands up in the stirrup much of the time. Camel stirrups are more like western stirrups, oblong and light.*

*Saws are generally kept above the door of the ger, in order to protect against any evil that might come through the door. Usually there is one, in this case two: double strength for double protection. The door is turquoise blue, the roof-rods of the ger are fire-engine red.*

*Darimaa's son, Ganhuik, is feeding this baby goat with a homemade milkbottle made from a goat-horn. A rubber nipple has been fitted to the end of the horn. Baby goats are often brought into their ger when very small and fed in this way.*

### GOATHERDER: *Sunjidmaa*

*S* *unjidmaa lives in a small community of six gers. The group moves as a unit when it is time to change pasture for the goats. Each ger is occupied by an average of six people, so the population of the community is about thirty-five, including children.*

*A police car has been visiting the community just before we arrive. The policeman announces that he is searching for a 'criminal,' and the atmosphere among the gers is tense. The car soon leaves, however, and smiles are considerably broader once the police are gone.*

*Many of the people in this part of the Gobi are of 'xarchin' stock, a particular ethnic group that is different from the main Khalkh majority in Mongolia. The word xarchin is derived from 'xar,' or black: the occupation of the xarchin used to be milking black horses for milk.*

*Sunjidmaa's ger is the one on the left, with the drying goat skin. In front of the ger are baskets for collecting argal. A shed for protecting the animals is to the north, the animal shelter in turn protecting the humans from the north wind.*

*This prayer flag came from the 'hiid' or temple at the local sum center. The flag has been shredded by the Gobi wind, which allows the prayers on it, written in the Tibetan script, to be released into the air. Common throughout Tibet, Bhutan, and Mongolia, such prayer flags predate Buddhism and can be traced to a more ancient Bon religion.*

*Sundjidmaa's daughter (left), one of her sons and another child on top of a Mongolian pony.*

*Sunjidmaa's daughter stands in front of an urga, or a pole with a loop on the end of it for catching animals. Her felt boots are common footwear among both children and adults in this part of the Gobi.*

## DRAWER OF WATER IN THE GOBI

*W*ells have existed throughout the Gobi for centuries, perhaps millenia. It is believed that the weather in this part of the world changed in the middle of the second millenium BC, and that the pastoral tradition followed an earlier, sedentary lifestyle in a warmer and wetter Mongolia.

*Wells are called 'khodag' in Mongolian and are marked on old maps of the Gobi; even today, many place names in the Gobi are the names of old wells. During the Russian period, many of these wells were fortified with cement structures and supplied with a circular 'arm' for pumping up the water.*

*This well is an older variety: water is drawn up in a bucket by hand and poured into the adjoining trough. This strong lady was drawing water in a heavy wind, pulling the rubber bucket up hand-over-hand to water her cows.*

*Miles from anywhere or anybody, she was wearing bougainvillea-pink lipstick. Gobi women are famous for their beauty. Since the harshness of life in the Gobi requires that people rely on one another, women there are also known for being hospitable, or 'saikhan setgel' in Mongolian.*

### GOBI OVOO

*A*n ovoo is a ritual pile of stones or objects that marks a sacred place. It is generally situated on a high spot, where one can survey the landscape and where herders, in particular, come to study the weather patterns and look for their flocks. The same basic word is spelled and pronounced differently in Mongolia, Tibet, China, Buryatia, and elsewhere in Central Asia, and the shapes and styles of ovoos also differ.

*right: A horsehead graces the top of an ovoo. Note the goat horns attached to the skull on the left. The ceremonial cloths, or khadag, are sky blue.*

*below: Looking down from an ovoo: the Gobi just before a snowstorm.*

*The bronze Buddha placed on this ovoo had probably been salvaged from a destroyed temple. Of the seven hundred monastery complexes in the country at the beginning of the century, only three remain. The rest were razed during the 1930s. The tradition of ovoos long predates Buddhism, which first entered Mongolia late in the thirteenth century and was reintroduced more successfully in the sixteenth.*

*right: This hiid, or temple, is just five years old, from the post-Russian period. It stands in the small town that forms the center of Gurvan Saikhan sum. Before the temple is an ancient shamanist symbol, the central axis through which spirits communicate with this world. Wooden posts, like the one seen here juxtaposed against a Buddhist temple, can also be seen beside derelict Christian churches in Buryatia, due north in Siberia. The more ancient beliefs and practices continue in both places.*

*below: Scattered around this ovoo are 'shagai,' the knucklebones of sheep, which are used in a multitude of Mongolian games as well as in divination. Bronze and sometimes silver replicas of these shagai have been found in bronze-age tombs dating to the first millenia BC; the tradition is thousands of years old but still quite alive.*

PROFESSIONAL WOMEN

ANTHROPOLOGIST: *Tumen*

I am an anthropologist. My field of study has been the origins of the ancient nomadic populations of Mongolia. I've studied this mainly from a paleoanthropological perspective.

What does that mean? Well, my research mostly involves examining human skulls. I evaluate the morphological differences, the teeth, the bones, the characteristics that indicate what type of human population the person belonged to.

The data is primarily from the first and second millenium BC, also some earlier sites from the neolithic period. To date, archaeologists have located around five hundred paleolithic sites in Mongolia, but none of these has yielded human remains. Any bones have been animal bones. One of the most important paleolithic sites is Tsagaan Agui, a cave in Bayanhongor aimag that appears to have been inhabited for many hundreds of thousands of years. I worked there myself earlier. No human remains have shown up yet: it will be spectacular news when they do.

Yes, I excavate also—that is to say, I take part in excavations. I have physically 'dug' in the past, but mainly I plan an excavation and keep clear documentation of the process. To give an example: in western Mongolia, we worked on a site that produced what is now known as the Chandaman Culture. The site is in Uvs aimag, around twenty kilometers from the city of Ulaanborn. The strata at the site go down to paleolithic times, but I worked on a section that dates from around the seventh to third century BC or what we call late Bronze Age to early Iron Age.

Chandaman is a very rich complex. We found many 'animal-style' plaques, knives, different decorative motifs on ceramics. Some very interesting anthropological processes took place on our territory in antiquity. From this site it's clear that there was a diverse mixture of Mongoloid and Indo-European populations at the time. The skulls of the two groups of people are different; the grave objects are different.

We have seen this mixing of east and west mainly in western Mongolia. Eastern Mongolia is not the same. There you find no mixing and the human skeletal remains are homogeneous throughout. Both Central and Eastern Mongolia appear to have been inhabited by Mongoloid peoples from the earliest times.

I recently founded a new Department at the University, so right now I am rather busy. I'm head of the Department of Anthropology and Archaeology at the Academy of Sciences, and also head of the new Department of Anthropology at the National University.

At the Institute *[History Institute of the Academy of Sciences]* I have about eight researchers. Three are post-grad students preparing their dissertations. Two of these study the physical development of Mongolian children living in different ecological and geographic zones around the country. Another studies the physical development of Mongolian children in urban areas.

Another of my students studies paleoanthropological materials from the aspect of paleopathology. That is to say, looking at ancient skeletal material to research ancient diseases. She uses x-ray analysis, and we are only now beginning to do DNA analysis. We are developing a program of joint research with Cambridge University in England, so my graduate student is there right now.

Naturally, DNA analysis is difficult in Mongolia because of the economic situation. We haven't had the chance to do all we need to do. In 1994 I visited Cambridge and also London University, and set up agreements for carrying on this research. I haven't been to America. I would like to make contact with Americans in this field, but have not yet had that pleasure.

The focus of my own research has been cranialogical study. As chief of the cranialogical mission I've done comparative analysis of different ethnic groups in western Mongolia, in particular. For the past ten years, I've been studying contemporary Mongolian populations. There are around twenty distinct ethnic groups in this country. Hovd aimag in the west has the largest concentration of different ethnic groups in any one area. Around ten ethnic groups are located there. For three years, I have been focusing on eastern Mongolia, with Korean researchers. For my doctoral dissertation, I did a comparative analysis with

*Tumen's study of skull morphology has demonstrated the extent of early Europoid immigration into western Mongolia. 'Early' in this sense means third to second millenia* BC.

neighboring Asian populations and also native American populations. With very interesting results, that I hope to publish one day.

How did I get started on this line of work? I graduated from the Moscow State University in anthropology because that is what the government told me to study. Twenty, thirty years ago, we could not choose our own subjects. Before the government sent me to study it, I had no idea what paleoanthropology was.

My salary is 34,000 tugriks per month from the Institute. From the University I get 16,000 tugriks, since there is a rule in the country that if you work for two state organizations you can only take half the salary in one of them. *[The total comes to around* US$100 *per month.]*

Financing our research is difficult. In Mongolia there is only one source of funding—the Science & Technology Foundation, which is a government foundation. All research grants, for the entire country, come from this organization. As a result, very little comes down to us, of course.

The main thing I would like to see is more research in molecular anthropology. For that, we need equipment. My biggest problem is getting funding for this equipment, and also for communications. The Academy of Sciences has exactly one computer linked to email, so it is hard to get access to it. Many scholars from other countries are interested in the subject of the origins of Mongolian populations. Other countries have been carrying out DNA research. But in Mongolia such investigation is impossible.

The political changes have been difficult. The years 1990 through 1992 were, in fact, very difficult. Also, one unfortunate consequence has been that almost all personal relationships with Russians were destroyed. We didn't merely sever political ties with Russia.

On the other hand, the changes have given many of us more opportunities—me for example. And every Mongolian now feels independent. Democracy has given us another immediate benefit: we can now contact anybody, from any country at all. Anyone who wants to come to Mongolia can do so. Before, this was impossible for western scholars to visit.

Yes, I participated in the founding of the Women's Association for Science and Technology. About half of Mongolian scientists are women. Women work in all academic institutes, in all fields. They carry out research in nuclear physics, biotechnology...some of our Mongolian women scientists are impressive. None is at the top of a department or an institute, however. All directors of institutes are men. There is a barrier to advancement and to participation in decision making. Equality between men and women in Mongolian science is a problem.

In the last five years, science has been poorly funded and the situation for women has deteriorated even more than for men. Women needed to organize to meet the aim of supporting their research. So last summer we organized a symposium on women in science and technology. All participants recommended setting up an association. To an extent, it's working. It provides a forum for discussion and, we hope, a way for the younger women in particular to contact western scholars in their fields.

I'm not interested in going into politics. Two years ago I was asked to run for Parliament. For a month I attended meetings, learned all about the process. And I realized that I am not a politician. I am a scientist, and I want to use the specialized knowledge and experience that I already have.

*As we leave the Ulaanbaatar Hotel, where we have been having lunch, Tumen says,* You know, five years ago, I could not have walked into this hotel. It was reserved for foreigners. Now, free!

*She opens her hands in a broad gesture in the crisp air. Fresh new snow is falling.*

### THE BEE LADY: *Selenge*

*S*elenge is known in Mongolia as the Bee Lady. She lives in a small
town two hours north of Ulaanbaatar. Russian buildings line the
*two or three unpaved streets. This community was originally built to
serve the railroad that passes nearby.*

*Now there are no Russians here, only crumbling buildings and impov-
erished Mongolians. The economy in this area depended heavily on
state-financed dairy production. The dairy is now closed, and of the one
thousand households in the neighborhood one quarter are classified as
'poor' and one tenth are 'very poor.'*

*Selenge, however, does not look poor. She is wearing a red sweater and
skirt, her hair is pulled back in a bun behind her head, emphasizing her
warm face and lovely, creamy skin. We meet in her office, which has
large windows facing the mountains across the valley.*

*Following my gaze, she says,* Those mountains are where the bees make
our honey.

How did I get started in this business? Well, first, I was born in Zavhan
aimag, a rather poor aimag to the northwest. But I was raised in Ulaanbaatar and went to high school there. I thought I might like to be a
doctor and I started out as a pre-med student.

Back then, perhaps you know, the government made the decisions
for us—who would go to Russia, who would study here in Mongolia.
The best students were given the opportunity to study abroad, and I
was one of the best. I was sent to Moscow.

At that time, nobody in Mongolia knew a thing about apiculture.
There was no information at all. People advised me to take it up,
saying that if I went into this field I would be the only woman in
Mongolia working with bees. I thought that would be an advantage
and so I decided to pursue it.

I stayed in Moscow for seven years. First I attended the Timeriazov
Academy, then, after graduation, I worked with Russian scientists.
Finally I brought a select group of bees back to Mongolia.

How did I bring them back? In a small box. At first, I brought only thirty bees. They multiplied here in Mongolia and we started production. The Ministry of Agriculture contributed to this effort and encouraged me to set up a small science center for research. That's how my work with bees got started.

*She motions to an assistant and soon small saucers of honey are brought in. We spoon the honey into our mouths, eating it directly, enjoying the flavor of wild flowers. The taste is much stronger than processed, store-bought honey.*

For the first ten years, I studied various kinds of bees and worked hard to isolate those qualities that would help the bees acclimatize to the Mongolian environment. During those years, I needed workers as well as technology, so I started a training center within this science center.

In 1959, the first real bee farm was started in Mongolia. There had been beekeeping before but not a centralized research facility. Russians had brought bees in, and kept them for a few years, but the effort dwindled and the bees died. There was no documentation, no record of the research. People in our country had not studied apiculture in a systematic way. But gradually, when I began to show how profitable this endeavor could be, people took an interest.

During this process I started promoting beekeeping on television, on the radio, in publications. And I found an enthusiastic reception. I went everywhere, talking, lecturing, and people were extremely helpful. For instance, the governor of this aimag was a great support. After I began lecturing at the university in Ulaanbaatar, a number of students began research programs in apiculture.

Then I was invited to come run this science center. Since I had given lectures to many students, I had access to the best talent and I brought them here and gave them jobs. I also was able to position my students in useful places. Right now I have more than ten students from the Agricultural College and the Teachers' University working in senior positions in the agricultural and environmental ministries. They remember me and have helped me a lot.

In 1989, I became a Doctor of Science in Apiculture. By that time I had developed a new variety of bee that is specially suited to the extremes of Mongolian weather. This new bee has been given the name of Lalyon, which is also my daughter's name. It's well adapted to intense cold, high altitudes, and dryness. We have distributed it to a number of aimags around the country, including Arkhangai, Hovd, Uvs, Selenge, Hintei, and Dornod.

*She has become animated, talking about her bee proselytizing. Now she turns to the subject of the future, and the subject of money.*

There are two main directions in which I want to take this Center in the future. First, we need more research on the medicinal and nutritional uses of honey, partly as a way to finance our efforts. Second, we need to work on developing disease-resistant strains and to create more sanitary conditions in the hives. For this second effort, I have enough hands-on experience myself, but I need technical expertise in veterinarian science. My daughter is now studying bees at the

Agricultural University, and I'm hoping that she will pursue this second direction in the future.

For money, we are developing products out of honey. Right now we are collecting between one and three tons of honey each year. We collect it right here in this facility but the beekeepers and hives are all out around the mountains.

Our main problem in selling honey is the packaging. As of now we don't export; we sell only within Mongolia and it's hard to get the right kind of glass jars. My dream is to have a packaging facility and to sell both within Mongolia and abroad.

Now people know about and want honey. At the beginning, it was a hard fight. Since it was a Socialist system, the government needed persuading in order to support the initial costs. They would say, "We have ten million sheep, we have ten million cows. Why do we need bees? What's the benefit? Only you, Selenge, will use this honey!" But I didn't give up. I told them, "You will become older. You will want this honey. You will have children who will want honey."

It was not a traditional Mongolian occupation to keep bees. Before, only a few people knew about this marvellous substance. Now, when Mongolians are sick, they say, "I need honey!"

We are also creating cosmetic products that utilize honey. I believe that the addition of honey to lanolin creates a cream that has lasting benefits for the skin. We all know about Pond's cream here, yet we find that we use it once and then need to apply it again the next day. Our skin stays dry. Using the cream I have developed, after I've used it twice my face becomes soft and stays soft. We've also learned that using a mask of honey and eggyolk is very beneficial for the skin. You use one spoon of honey and one yolk of egg, mix this up and pat it on your face. Leave it on for fifteen to twenty minutes and then rinse it off with water. You can also add a little vegetable oil.

Now I must speak of our poverty. In this part of the country in particular it is very bad. I am working to develop a 'Women and Bee Farming' program. We are trying to resolve the unemployment problem here. A large number of households are headed by women; that is, the man has either gone to the city, or the woman has been divorced or abandoned. I love our Mongolian women, and I want to help them. I am trying to have them trained here, so they can under-stand the profits of beekeeping. Everywhere in the world, women help each other. Women are the ones who must carry their families. They all know and undertand this.

We have not yet completed the planning stages, but we are hoping to develop the program in three areas: first, in training women to run small-scale bee farms, second in training women in the production of honey once it is gathered, and third in organizing a health and beauty spa that utilizes honey in its products.

I believe that beekeeping is particularly suited to women. They can do it in the summer, not in the winter when the weather is severe outside the ger. You know that bees work only on good days, on sunny days. On bad days, when the weather is cruel, they too stay inside.

One last thing: bee farms are good for our Mongolian nature. They are clean, they pollinate flowers. They contribute to the environment. Wherever our bees go, that place becomes more beautiful. Ecologists know this. I now find it impossible to think about nature without our bees.

*She blows me a kiss when I leave. She is both graciously European, and a strong Mongolian woman.*

*Child belonging to one of the poorer families in Selenge's somon.*

PHYSICIAN: *Oyuntsetseg*

*O yuntsetseg is a stylish woman, blue beret, gold earrings, modish rag haircut. She smiles easily but is also reserved, with a contemplative look about her.*

When I was in the eighth or ninth grade I began to think about what I would do in life. The choice for me was between linguist and doctor. The Ministry of Education had a quota for higher education at that time: each subject was to receive a certain number of students. This quota included a fixed number of fellowships to study in Russia.

No fellowships were being offered for linguists. There were, however, some for doctors, which were granted on the basis of one's marks on qualifying exams. I took the exams and had high marks, so I passed.

I left for Russia at the age of seventeen. I attended the Institute of Medicine in Irkutsk, just to the west of Lake Baikal. In Mongolia I had studied chemistry, biology, and so on—what you would call premed in America. The system of preliminary training in Mongolia was similar to that in Russia, so I was prepared to go straight into medicine. Our system includes six years of medical education, five of which are general and the sixth of which is in a specialization. My specialization at that time was internal medicine.

Once I graduated, the Ministry of Health assigned me to a posting. The Ministry had a system of allocating personnel to hospitals according to the needs of the hospital and the abilities of the candidate. Students trained in Russia rated quite high, so I was offered a position at Hospital Number One, the best in Mongolia. If I had been in cardiology I doubt if I could have got into Hospital Number One. Cardiology was very popular and the competition was stiff.

The Hospital had a vacancy for a kidney specialist. So they decided to train me in kidney disease. I worked closely with Russian specialists at the hospital and then was sent for a further two years of training in Bulgaria. I studied at the Medical Academy in Sophia.

After finishing the training in Sophia, I was allowed to work as a kidney specialist on my own, back in Ulaanbaatar. The nephrology department in Hospital Number One has fifty beds and five doctors.

It has the only dialysis equipment in the country. I worked as head of the department from 1990.

I worked in that hospital for fifteen years altogether, from 1980, first as assistant, and then as chief. But with the change in government, the situation there has deteriorated. There is no money and it is very disturbing to see people unable to get appropriate treatment. The equipment has broken down and people are dying needlessly.

We need to inform the Prime Minister, the President, about these problems. Something has to be done, but the situation is beyond the power of a single person. It requires more than just professional skills and expertise. The low salaries and high cost of living have also led to low morale of the staff. Nobody is working. As a responsible person I have found it hard to run an operation that is not at all professional.

Also, I have a family to help support. My salary is 15,000 tugriks per month, around $30. My rent now approaches $200 per month. Until recently, there were food shortages, and we spent a lot of time standing in lines. There was severe rationing. Then finally products started coming in. This eliminated the lines but prices went up dramatically.

And so I am quitting the hospital and opening a clinic on my own. I feel I can do more to carry out preventive medical treatment by opening a private practice and working on early diagnosis and prevention. At the clinic, people were admitted only if they were in critical stages of kidney disease, when it was already too late. If they could have been treated at an earlier stage it would have been far better.

There is no preventive medical care in Mongolia, partly because of the overall shortage of doctors. So I have decided to go on my own. It will benefit more people and I can also earn more as a private doctor.

Do I need permission to do this? Yes, opening a clinic requires approval from the Ministry of Health. You have to get special authorization, which I have done.

How does insurance work here? Starting from January 1994, all people are covered by medical insurance. Before then, medical care was free for all. Now it is not. Parliament has adopted laws but so far private practice is not covered by any insurance payments. So everyone is supposed to pay fees.

If a patient needs to be hospitalized, I transfer them to the hospital and the patient is then covered by insurance. But if you have been to Hospital Number One, you will see that it is under great pressure. It is not easy to get medical treatment there.*

Kidney disease is a big problem here in Mongolia. This is related first to our climate, second to a diet including a lot of meat, and third, also perhaps to a great deal of gynecological disease. Venereal diseases are very common.

Another big problem here is that women are pregnant very many times. They lack or do not use contraceptives. As a result, there is a tremendous amount of aborting of children in Mongolia. I would say that, on average, each woman has three to four abortions. Some many more.

This figure applies to urban women. In the countryside, women just give birth. Before, contraceptives and abortion were discouraged, or shall we say forbidden. If you had five children or more you were allowed to apply for an abortion. This so-called 'democratic policy' of forbidding abortions led to illegal abortions, malpractice, and many deaths. The policy was changed only four years ago.

Am I hopeful? No, in terms of medical care I am not very hopeful. The situation will get much worse before it gets better. I will simply do what I can.

*\* A visit to Hospital Number One is an illuminating experience. The halls are lined with people; families sleep outside rooms that are packed with patients. The hospital is serving people from the countryside in particular, and the lack of hygiene is apparent. Doctors occasionally walk by in off-white coats, giving a reassuringly medical look to the bizarre scene, but the systems have basically broken down.*

### MUSEUM CURATOR: *Shinebayar*

*S*hinebayar is curator at the local museum in the town of Mandalgobi in the Middle Gobi aimag. Mandalgobi was one of the strategic points for the Russian military presence in Mongolia. Now that the Russians have pulled out, the population of the town is less than 10,000 and the town is struggling to reestablish its identity. The area around town housed a large arsenal as well as the Russian military personnel. Mounds of dirt lie to the south, where weaponry was removed. Such mounds are not unique to Mandalgobi: one of the largest sites is some fifty kilometers southwest of Ulaanbaatar, where nuclear weapons were stored.

I was born in Mandalgobi. My parents were born in the countryside, in Gurvan Saikhan somon, but my father moved to this town as a young man. My grandfather and great grandfather were herdsmen in the Gobi. Why did my parents move to town? Because, like all parents, they were concerned about the future of their children.

I attended primary and secondary school here in Mandalgobi. My teachers were all Mongolian, although there was a Russian school that some Mongolians could attend. You know, there was a sizeable Russian presence here. Most of the military personnel lived outside of town, in a separate 'Russian village.' There were also a number of Russians living inside Mandalgobi but they were what we called 'experts,' such as agricultural advisors. All of the Russian children attended their own Russian school. I talked to them sometimes: I had a few friends who were Russians and of course we always spoke in Russian, but I myself attended a Mongolian school.

What was it like with the Russians here? Nowadays it doesn't matter but back then many of us really did believe that Russia was our big brother. We were made to think of Mongolia as the little brother. They had considerable strength to make us feel this way. After the Revolution [1921], Russians and Mongolians had to live together, to work towards the future together as brothers. The symbol of that brotherhood is on the monument at the top of the hill north of town: a Russian hammer and sickle and the Mongolian *soyombo* symbol. *Drushba* is the Russian word for it, *nairamdal* is the Mongolian word for it: friendship.

*We are sitting in one of the two functioning rooms in the main hotel in town. The rest of the rooms have broken windows or are bare of furniture. There are two functioning toilets in the hotel as well, which means that you can pour water into them after use and the water will go down an unplugged drain. The water must be brought to the toilet in a bucket. Shinebayar has been camping with us in the countryside. This is mid-May, but we arrive back in town in the midst of a blizzard and are glad to have a roof over our heads.*

I couldn't say exactly how many Russians were in the Russian village, but there was a large Russian division here. The arsenal had tanks, rockets; there was a radar station. Nuclear weapons I don't know about.

After graduation from secondary school I attended the Culture College in Ulaanbaatar. I knew that I wanted to return and work in the local museum here, so I graduated with a degree in museum science.

The Local Museum of Middle Gobi Aimag has a staff of eleven people. It is a national-level museum, so its budget comes from the central government, from the Ministry of Culture. Needless to say, the budget is very small.

My salary is 15,000 tugriks per month [$30]. It's enough for me. Salaries and overhead and so on are not our main problem. What the museum needs most is funding for doing research on its collections and for purchasing new objects.

Why buy more things? We were restricted before in what we could purchase. It was a political decision. For example, a man wanted to bring us a geneological study of people in this region—it was a very important thing, but we couldn't take it. Until five years ago, the government here was very political. It was impossible to allow anything that might be too 'nationalistic' to be brought into the museum.

Nowadays things are different, but now there is not enough material left in Mongolia to understand our past.

Most of the objects collected for our museum were from the distant past. Yes, such as the fossilized sea-horses, but also bronze artefacts from around two thousand years ago. Our museum has the best collection of bronze artefacts in the country. The reserves, what we call

the 'Fund,' was gathered in three different ways: some objects were presented to us, some we bought, and some were collected in scientific expeditions.

Around twenty percent of the Museum's collection used to be political, such as portraits of Lenin and so on. It was a small percentage but an important part of exhibitions. We've changed the exhibitions now. We've put up Mongolian artefacts and we have some very interesting objects still in storage. But we now need to research what they are. People now want to know more about their own history and tradition. They have to see artefacts, to realize what happened here on this very land, from dinosaurs to kings. People want to know.

*page 155: Shinebayar stands by Yarkh Uul in the Gobi, holding a small blue Siberian iris, one of the first wildflowers of spring in the Gobi. The small, ancient mountain called Yarkh Uul is in Shinebayar's native sum, Gurvan Saikhan, where it stands alone, a high point in the middle of the desert. A hallowed place, it is still once a year the site of ceremonial offerings by the local people. Mongolians do not say the name of a sacred mountain, but rather call all sacred mountains by the word 'khairkhan,' or holy peak. There is evidence of paleolithic as well as neolithic occupation of this site: early hominids fashioned their stone tools here for hundreds of thousands of years.*

*preceding page:*
*top: Mandalgobi from the north, looking east toward the gers of the Mongolian part of the town.*
*bottom: From the same ovoo, looking west toward the now-defunct Soviet industrial part of town. The ovoo is one of many on top of this hill: an old map in the museum shows ovoos once ringing the area. Each ovoo on the map had the name of the person who was to tend it written next to it in old Mongolian script.*

*Museum Director Munhbyar. She stands in front of a display case with bronze artefacts dating from the first centuries* BC*, collected from the local aimag. Her museum houses the finest collection of bronze artefacts in the country.*

*One of the many defunct 'building materials' factories in Mandalgobi. The doors of the factory are painted flamingo pink.*

*A statue in the main square of Mandalgobi, across from the school.*

## GETTING STARTED IN BUSINESS

### CRAFTSWOMAN IN ZUNMOD: *Purevsuren*

*Purevsuren lives in the city of Zunmod, capital of Tov or Central aimag, in a new district called Bayanhoshoo.*

I've lived in this district for almost five years, since this little one here was born. Before, my husband and I had an apartment in one of the buildings in town. Both of us were salaried employees, but when the government changed, state enterprises stopped paying the salary.

So we were told to come out here and build ourselves a place to live. Our old apartment was then given to others. This whole Bayanhoshoo area is new—all the wooden shacks you see here date from four to five years ago.

It hasn't been easy, this transition to a market economy. Would I rather live down there? Of course I would. You have running water, heat, and you don't have to build the place yourself. For example, in an apartment you also have a toilet. Here we go outside, and in winter it is cold. The heat inside our house here is actually better than in an apartment, with our stove. We mainly use wood and dung to keep the place warm, also some charcoal.

Did we just select a piece of land to build on and build there? Oh no. The government said this is where you are to build. We couldn't just build anywhere. Yes, the land is free and belongs to the country, but that doesn't mean that people can just use it as they want. No, we didn't pay for this plot of land. We were told that this was our allocation, and so we built here. We understand that a new law has been passed and that from next year we may have to start paying land rent. We don't yet know how much, but that's a little worrying too.

I have two daughters, and my husband is an artist as well. I mentioned that the transition has not been easy, but I want to emphasize that, before, I never really thought about anything. I just did the paintings I was told to paint and took my salary. When our country started to change to a market economy, I had to think for myself. I realized I had to do some kind of business, to make some money to survive.

I got started in my business by making the little clay gers that you see here. These are my own design.

I made a few, and took them up to Manz'shir, the old monastery near here up in the mountains. It's destroyed and abandoned, but visitors come, and I thought I might be able to sell them. And in fact I sold some. I went by myself and just introduced myself to the keepers of the place who live in the gers. After that they kept on buying a few from time to time.

Soon, though, I was too tired to keep it up. It took me a long time to get up there, for very little profit. I realized I had to find a better outlet. Since then I have been selling through the Department Store in Ulaanbaatar. I have to transport the products myself, of course, which takes both time and money. Ulaanbaatar is around an hour from here. But I make a little money from it; I have the model gers, and also these wall hangings and a few little paintings. I probably make around 20,000 to 30,000 tugriks per month [$40 to $60]. It depends on the season: there are visitors in summer, but no one buys in winter.

Actually, this is not enough to live on. For example, I need to prepare for winter. I need to buy wood and coal for heating, also clothes and food for my children. Tax? Yes, the government takes tax out of what I earn. I get the money through the bank, not directly from the store, so right away they take out 20%.

I sell each model ger to the department store for 200 tugriks. The department store sells them to the customer for 250. So I bring home 200 less the tax, or 160 tugriks for each [$0.35]. How many have I sold? Oh! That's very hard to say. I may have sold a total of 1,000 since the beginning [total income from the gers around $350].

For the future, I need to find more places to sell. I know I could improve my marketing and I'm interested in trying. I approve of the transition to a market economy, but if I can't find a market for my products, it will be bad.

These are my two daughters; that other little girl is a friend, not mine. I say two is enough. I don't want any more. When my two daughters go to school and, I hope, to university, they will need money. So I take some medicine in order not to have more children. I sincerely hope that my two daughters will be able to get an education.

*The older daughter is studying English in her school. I ask her age and she says, with perfect pronunciation, "I am eight years old."*

*Bayanhosho, the rapidly growing district outside Zunmod, where Purevsuren was told to build herself a new home.*

*page 163: Purevsuren with her two daughters in front of their home. "Two is enough."*

### SHOP-OWNER IN AMGALANT: *Chimge*

*C*himge runs a shop in one of the gertowns of Ulaanbaatar, one of
*the spreading districts of wooden shacks and felt gers that ring the
city. There is nothing but foot traffic in her neighborhood, along the dirt
roads and small paths winding between fenced-in yards. Her shop is in
the corner of a one-story building. A very small sign on top of the
building says 'Food Store' in Mongolian.*

*To get to her shop, you take a tram to the end of the line, going east from
Ulaanbaatar. You walk across an open field, crawl through a fence, jump
across a couple of small ditches and pass a cabbage field. Once you get to
the shacks, you head into the thick of them and look for the most solidly
constructed building.*

*Chimge is around 35. She moves with vigor into a discussion of her life.*

I was actually trained as a doctor. After graduation I worked five or
six years in a hospital. When the economy changed I started looking
for something to do to survive.

My sister, brother and I began with a flour operation. I started like a
man, carrying sacks of flour with my brother.

After that, I began to make bread and then cakes. The idea of having
a shop came when we first started making bread: once we had made
it, we wondered how we were going to sell it. That was around three
years ago. The capital for the first lot of goods came from selling flour.
My brother helped at the start; now I'm running the business alone
with my younger sister.

Where do we get things to sell? All over. It may look easy, but it isn't.
I have to go everywhere to find things and to see what the situation is
in other shops. I need to be completely knowledgeable about pricing.
Since we don't want to hire anyone, we do everything ourselves.

We go to market, buy food, bring it back and sell it. Sometimes I
go to the big open-air market.* Some products we buy directly from
the factories. Mostly flour, bread, rice—food that Mongolians use
every day.

How much stock I keep on hand depends on the product, but we generally restock around twice a week. Since we carry everything to the shop ourselves by hand—we have no lorry—we can only buy in small amounts. I hope to buy a car in the future. A Lada's the car for me. A used one costs around 250,000 tugriks [$500].

The economics of the business are like this: one kilo of flour costs me 90 tugriks and I sell it for 110 tugriks. So I make 20 tugriks per kilo [$.04]. Flour has three grades: 90-tugrik flour is the middle grade and I get a price break on it from the people who make it. If I had to buy from the market I would pay 118 tugriks and would have to sell at 130. There wouldn't be much market here for that.

Every day I sell 100 or 140 kilos. It's sold in two sizes of bags, 50 or 70 kilos, and usually I sell two bags a day. So I make 2,000 tugriks a day off flour, on average [around $4]. Not bad.

However, sometimes nobody buys. People buy more during the holidays, but now Naadam* is over. Before Tsagaan Sar, Mongolian New Years, I sell special cakes. *She demonstrates how big they are with her hands, around seven inches across.* Very beautiful. Every family buys at least one.

We live in an apartment in Ulaanbaatar and take the tram out every morning. I get up at eight a.m. and go to bed around ten or eleven in the evening. The store closes at seven but I stay on to finish the work. State stores, of course, open from eleven a.m., although they are supposed to open at nine, and they take lunch break from one to three. Then they close at six in the evening. I open at ten, take no lunch break, and close at seven.

Why out here? Getting a store inside Ulaanbaatar is expensive, and difficult to find. This place is good. Of course, I dream of opening a big store in Ulaanbaatar one day.

*The largest store in Ulaanbaatar is the State Department Store. Every morning there are long lines of people on the ground floor, queuing to buy butter and bread. How does the price of bread in this government-operated state store relate to the price of bread in her little shop?*

Here's how it works, at least right now. People buy state-produced bread at the State Department Store, and then resell it in other parts of the city. Butter is the same way. The Department Store is like a wholesale distribution outlet, and the price of their bread is still controlled, so it's lower.

The government subsidizes bread produced in state factories, so their price for one loaf is 90 tugriks. If I buy their bread for resale, by law I am only allowed to raise the price up to 150%. If someone makes bread himself and sells it, he can set his own price.

Yes, I do buy bread from the state factories. How much do I raise the price? Generally 10 to 20%. Sometimes I make bread myself. I have a bread machine, made in Czechoslovakia, that bakes thirty loaves at a time. But the profit is not as high as when I make cake, and in this area people now mostly buy cake from me.

The tax rate is 30% of my profits, every three months. We are supposed to pay four times a year, so we need to keep very clear accounts. Does anyone come to check? Generally not, but occasionally they do. This place is like 'countryside.' Government people don't much like to come out here. In the center of Ulaanbaatar, on the other hand, they come every day. There they have much tighter control.

People are fewer out here. There aren't so many customers to begin with and their income is low. In fact, most people in this area are unemployed. Most keep their own sheep and cattle; some do a little trading business. People in this gertown are either old or very young.

One other reason I'm here is that my sister's husband is in charge of the company that owns the building. So I don't have to pay rent. There are nine children in our family and we all help each other.

My parents? My father died when my mother was 32.

*Nine children before the age of 32?*

Yes, my mother was married at sixteen and had a child every year or so after that. Before my father died, my mother didn't have to work. Father was a driver, which was a job with high pay. He went many places, was able to travel, and he would come home and say, 'when my children grow up they must get a higher education.' He dreamed of his children becoming professionals. So my mother did everything she could for us. After father died, she started working. She made clothes in a factory. She worked all day every day, then brought home material to work on at night. She was such a hard worker, such a good example to everyone.

At that time Mongolian people were optimistic. They worked hard for their children and the future. My mother died in 1989...I can't help becoming emotional when I think about her.

*She is crying. Her eyes are red and, with no tissue, she uses her hands to wipe the tears off her cheeks.*

*\*The wholesale distribution of food in Ulaanbaatar takes place at a large open-air market to the north of the city.*

*\*Naadam is a festival of sporting events that include wrestling, archery, and horse racing. The national Naadam is generally held outside Ulaanbaatar in July; aimags and local areas are now also beginning to hold naadams.*

ENTREPRISING LADY: *Har Nuteng*

*H*ar Nuteng* is slender, with short permed hair and a ready smile. Her ger is comfortable, around twenty feet in diameter. Thirty loaves of broad are stacked on a side table, ready to sell in her shop.*

I am a very busy woman. We have land, goats, and a shop to take care of. *She says all this straight off, proud of her enterprise.*

I graduated from a university in Irkutsk, and worked for twenty-five years as a teacher of the Russian language. Several years ago, my husband and I decided to let our children use the apartment we had in the city; we moved out to live in a ger.*

So we looked for this small piece of land, for a place to raise our goats and some vegetables. In this transition to a market economy, we have had to think of several ways of making a living.

I have six children; two are university students, three are in secondary school. The oldest five are girls; my little son here came later. Milk is cheaper if you have your own animal, so we decided to buy our own goats. We bought four from the countryside, which my children tend. If we have more than enough milk for ourselves, we sell some to other families around. The vegetables we raise ourselves are enough for us each year. My husband generally buys meat for the winter out in the countryside where the price is lower.

My pension is 5,000 tugriks per month [$10]. It's not enough. With two daughters in university, we have to pay for the classes they want to take—each course costs money. In order to make some extra, we decided to open a little shop. It's not a difficult thing to do, but now, after doing it for a while, I realize how much time I have to spend on it. Every day I have to plan the work schedule. How many children can I use in the shop, who should herd the four goats, who will milk them, and so on. Actually I do most of the milking myself, but all of the children can milk. I've found that three of them are better at it than the others.

To open the shop I had to get various permissions from the State. Sanitary checkup, statement of financial condition and so on. I had

*Behind Har Nuteng are the framework and door of another ger.*

to go to the District office—for one month I did nothing but that. I opened the shop in June and it will close in September, when the children go back to school: they're the ones who sit behind the counter and sell things.

Then there's the vegetable plot to take care of. I worked to get this land for three years. A new law is being drafted in Mongolia about leasing of land. When it is passed, we will have to pay for the land, but we haven't paid anything yet.*

We bought this ger. We didn't make it. We had a family ger from my husband's parents, but it went to his brother. A good ger should last twenty to thirty years in its prime. Then it needs refurbishing, changing all the materials. We repaint the wood every few years, and also make new fabric covers for the inside.

My youngest brother and my sister's husband helped us build the shop.* The trouble with the shop is controlling the consumption of my children. I tell them that if they didn't eat our supplies we might have an income of 100,000 tugriks per month. It's the same with the bread. I made a contract with the little breadmaking company of a local family. I buy at 130 tugriks per loaf and I sell at 135 to 150 per loaf [profit per loaf is less than five cents]. But for every four loaves I buy, I give two to my children.

Fortunately my health is good. After four years of goat milk I'm much better—goat milk has more fat than cow milk and is good for older people. The milk is best from a mother goat who has just had a kid. But, you know, goats don't produce very much milk. You have to milk a goat twice a day anyway, like a cow, but you still get only around two liters.

How do I feel about the transition? When I was a teacher, I felt better. I had a salary every month, never mind how low. Also, my days were spent teaching children, which was good. I felt younger working with young people. But now I must think about my own children. I have to do it. The times are different.

*Har Nuteng's five-year-old son is a bright-eyed and happy young fellow, with a sweet smile. He sits by the little window of the shop, ready and willing to make a sale.*

*Her name means Black Eyes.

*Families who were allocated apartments by the previous government are trying to hold onto them. Once privatization occurs, they will hold a substantial asset. Some speculators are illegally buying apartments from others in anticipation of profit.

*As of this writing, it is uncertain how Mongolia is going to deal with the 'leasing' of property to individuals.

*The shop is four feet wide and about six feet long, made of wood.

## RESILIENCE

### HALF-RUSSIAN, HALF-MONGOLIAN: *Inna*

Yes, there is also alimony in this country, or rather what I would call child support. The law states that 10% of a man's salary should go to the wife for helping raise the children.

Take my husband as an example.* He has children by two different women before. He was not married to the first one, so he pays nothing to her. To the second he pays 10% of his monthly income. As a researcher in the Academy of Sciences, this is 20,000 tugriks per month. His former wife, in other words, gets 2,000 tugriks[$4]. It's a joke.

I don't think that divorce is a greater problem now than it used to be. It is true that social changes have been traumatic and relationships have suffered. But this is true everywhere and it was true here also before. I've been married twice; I have two children who are now 23 and 21. This little one here is by my second marriage.

There was a period in recent Mongolian history when it was, how shall we say, fashionable to have a Russian wife. Tsedenbal, the former president of the country, had a Russian wife.* Many prominent men had Russian wives.

They all knew each other. My mother used to come socialize with the Russian lady living here in your building, across the hall. Your neighbor's husband was a general; he died some years ago. Yes, the Russian wives stay on. What else can they do? It's no better in Russia. Here they have pensions, they have friends, their established routine.

But the world they lived in was a different world. My husband's father, for instance, taught history, the history of the Communist Party. He was quite respected. Of course he didn't actually believe in the history of the Communist Party. It didn't seem to matter, ethically, that one was teaching lies. It was a different world. You can't make judgments now about behavior back then. Now he's doing some kind of teaching in a private secondary school.

My salary is higher than my husband's. Also, the apartment we live in was given to us by the company I work for. Before, for six years, we lived with my husband's parents. It was awful. I was glad to be able to move out on our own. Even though we lived in a one-room flat I could at least breathe.

Many women are now supporting their families. The fact is that women are the ones doing the work and being hired to do even menial labor in Mongolia right now. You can see many construction teams out there, all women. Why? The men are unreliable. Yes, the men come to work today but who can say if they'll come tomorrow. Women are reliable.

Drinking among men is a problem, but it's not just alcoholism. Some Mongolian men are simply unreliable. I want to emphasize that I consider myself Mongolian. My mother was Russian and I was born in Moscow, but my life is here. I'm not going back to Russia. My family is spread around. My brother lives in Paris; my sister married a Hungarian and for the past twenty years has lived in Budapest. One other sister lives here in Mongolia. The situation in Russia is probably worse than here; at least, no better. I went back to visit Moscow last year, but nobody cares to go back there to live.

I can't say that I've felt any kind of backlash against Russians here. The Russians pulled out, but that has not affected people's attitudes towards me. We are all just trying to get along.

*Inna's husband is Mongolian. She is half-Mongolian, half-Russian.*

*It is said that Tsedenbal's wife essentially ran the country for his last ten years when he was senile.*

### TRACTOR DRIVER: *Mandakh*

*M*andakh's house outside Zunmod is not easy to find. It is tiny, more like a dog kennel. Through the fence her lot looks vacant.

*We enter the house through a door in the north, bending down to get in. It turns out to be sunk in the earth, so you can stand up inside. There are two miniature rooms, with beds, and the beds are made up and tidy.*

*Mandakh is thin with dyed black hair and straight-across bangs. Heavy lines of black eye shadow go all the way around her eyes. She looks like an experienced lady, and her manner is tough. Once she starts talking it is hard to stop her. It is soon obvious that this is an animated, spirited woman who has had a hard time in life but not been broken.*

I am 39 years old. How am I getting along? Well, so-so.

Before transition, my life was, how to say, well it was good. My profession was tractor driver. Yes, I worked as a tractor driver. It wasn't usual for a woman to do that, but I did. I graduated from the eighth grade in secondary school, and then worked as a state employee. So the salary was fine. I had enough. But when the open economy started, for two years it was very difficult.

First, my salary stopped. Also, I was in debt, so anything I made had to go to pay back my loans. Also, I changed my husband a few times. I couldn't seem to get along with any of them.

I felt everything was angry—life, people, my situation—it was all angry. I felt very bad at that time, but I just went on living.

After the government changed, some men took over the jobs with tractors. At the time, I wasn't unhappy about it. I was alone in being a female tractor driver. After my first child, my mother-in-law criticized me, said she hated my job. She said that I was a woman and a mother and should stay home and take care of things. I should have kept on being a tractor driver. If I still worked there, things would be different now. You know, sometimes parents tell us the wrong things.

Now? Well, I'm trying. Food prices are going up so quickly. I would like to be able to change my life as quickly, and adapt, but I just can't change as fast as I would wish.

In 1993, I was one of the women selected for the PO-5 project, growing vegetables. But I ate all that I grew the first year. This year I hope to store some, and sell them. I've been able to harvest 35 kilograms of carrots and 100 kilograms of potatoes. The price will be higher in spring, so I'll sell them then.

*How did it feel, driving a tractor across the wide steppe?*

I drove that tractor as hard as I could. I tried to become a 'hero of labor.' You see the different pictures of Lenin here on the walls. No, they are not just wall covering! I really believe in Lenin. We were taught about him in school, and he was the first good man I knew about. Also, here is Choibalsan and Sukhbaatar. These men did good things, strong things.

I have five children—two daughters and three boys. My oldest son is 23 and lives somewhere else. But he comes to help me. Soon he'll help me put up a winter ger in the yard. I was married a few times, although only once officially. None of my husbands gives me anything. I live on what I make myself.

In addition to the vegetables, I've tried to do a little selling of things on my own. Like animal skins, also *samar* nuts. You see people hawking them on the streets. My son goes into Ulaanbaatar to sell them. All in all, we're getting along.

*From time to time she becomes expressive, throwing her head back to let her voice ring out. Her mouth opens wide to laugh at herself. She is wiry and tough, with a raucous sense of humor.*

*Two young daughters hover nearby as we talk, one of whom proudly displays the coloring book she has done. The stories are unusual. One is about a man who goes to look for a magical deer that lives in a house. The man rides his horse to the house but finds that the deer has gone and that nine wolves are chasing it for their dinner. He sees the tracks of the wolves leading in the direction of his own house! He returns, to find that the wolves have failed—they are gone and the deer is back safely in its own home.*

*The moral of this little girl's tale is unclear, but it is apparent that she believes the story has a positive ending.*

*Mandakh proudly shows off two of her daughters, as well as her vegetables.*

DIPLOMAT: *Tumen*

I was born in Selenge aimag, in eastern Mongolia. At the age of one, my family and I moved to Ulaanbaatar. I am now sixty-five, so that was in the 1930s. I grew up here. I went to the 'Number One Secondary School,' yes, the best in the country.

Then, at the age of nineteen, I went to Moscow to study at the Institute of Oriental Studies. I concentrated in the Chinese language. My husband attended the Institute of International Relations where his degree was in international law and French. We were married after graduation.

In those days, many parents were unwilling to let their children go to Moscow. Only six students went in 1949; I was one of them. The train was rather different then. There was no food, no heat. And you had to catch it up at the border since it didn't come down this far. But it was an adventure. I was one of the earliest from Mongolia to study in Moscow, but I was not a member of the very first class—there were two before me, in 1947 and 1948. I was, however, the first woman to go to Moscow.

Before 1929, many students from Mongolia went to Germany. For example, the famous writer Natsagdorj studied there. These students brought back western culture and also western clothing. White shirt and tie, felt hats—these they wore with the traditional del, and the style has persisted among 'dandies' to this day.

After graduation, I went to work for the Ministry of Foreign Affairs. When I was twenty-seven years old, I was sent to China to serve in the Embassy. I stayed there three-and-a-half years. This was prior to the rupture between the Soviet Union and China, and Mongolia and China were still on friendly terms. I enjoyed my time in China, and I still enjoy the Chinese language.

Then my husband and I were posted to the United Nations in New York. I worked at the Permanent Mission of Mongolia in New York and he worked at the UN Secretariat. He was present at the first General Assembly meeting during which Mongolia was officially admitted to the UN. Those were exciting times, when Mongolia received

world recognition by being granted UN membership. Altogether, we spent ten years in New York.

When my husband was appointed Consul General in Leningrad and then, most recently, Ambassador to Algeria, I served in Protocol posts in those embassies as well.

Most of my professional life has been spent in the field of Protocol. This is very demanding in terms of time and duties. There are innumerable diplomatic ceremonies and procedures. You have to organize what happens when, who does what, and you have to be present at all functions. It is not an easy job for a woman with a family. Delegations generally have functions in the evening, and there was little time for children. But I tried to organize my life so that it could be done. I got up early to fix the day's food, then taught the children to cook for themselves when they got older. I believe this made them self-reliant, which I am glad for now. My oldest daughter cooked by herself at the age of eight. On Saturday I did all the work around the house; there was certainly no maid to help.

But the work has been interesting. I've met and hosted many famous people visiting our country, including the wife of the last Afghan King, who came with smelly suitcases and took baths in milk. Also Indira Gandhi in the 1960s, who came with Sanjay, her son. She was then Minister of Information, not yet Prime Minister. She was intelligent, modest, very laconic and thoughtful. She cooked for herself: I remember well that she preferred her own food.

Until 1989, most delegations were from socialist countries. I have met Brezhnev, Gorbachov, Tito, Zhou Enlai—all of them, here in Ulaanbaatar. In 1959, I watched Mao Zedong at the tenth anniversary of the victory of the Revolution. All the diplomats were lined up, watching, in Tiananmen Square. At that time, I was the only one in the Mongolian embassy who spoke Chinese. I also saw the Dalai Lama in Beijing in 1959. He was very young at the time, wearing his yellow hat.

To me, the Cultural Revolution began in China in 1961–62. We could already feel that the revolution would be coming in earnest.

Yes, I was a member of the Party. Not now. In 1991, the civil servants working in the Foreign Service were supposed to be 'impartial' as they pursued their duties. The Communist Party was no longer, of course, the government. And so the entire staff of the Foreign Ministry gave up Party affiliation. That is how we managed that aspect of the transition.

Now we have nineteen embassies here in Ulaanbaatar. With the UNDP [United Nations Development Program] and other international organizations, there are well over twenty representative bodies, so many more foreigners live here now than before. Now that I have retired, a friend and I have had time to help organize the International Ladies Association of Mongolia. The purpose has been to exchange experience among women of all countries and to help poor Mongolian women and children.

We meet once a month, we raise money, and we assist in projects that we feel are worthwhile. For example, we have organized a special refuge for street children in Ulaanbaatar. Seventy children are given food there, as well as some education. This has recently become a problem, since poor mothers who find out about it send their children to us. It is difficult to turn some away and take in others, but we don't have the resources to handle them all.

But somebody has to help. The government does not have resources at all to provide for the healthcare problems. Remote hospitals in particular are understaffed and underqualified. So another project this year has been to make donations of food to dormitories of schoolchildren in the remote aimags. These are herders' children, who gather to attend school in one location—the children live together since their homes are far from one another. The Association donates rye flour, sugar, and so on. Three doctors have also donated some services, an opthalmologist, a pediatrician, and a doctor in traditional medicine; all three are Mongolian women.

In 1992 we helped establish an orphans' center, with clothes and facilities for children, from newly born babies up to three-year-olds. Some of the women go regularly to help feed the children.

I was brought up in a socialist society and under the ideas of socialism. Now things are undergoing a political transformation, moving toward a market economy. The transition is difficult but I am optimistic. Good things are happening in Mongolia. The mentality is positive.

# POSTSCRIPT

## MEMBER OF PARLIAMENT: *Narangerel*

*O*n *June 30, 1996, national elections were held in Mongolia. Citizens were asked to choose their representatives for Parliament, the governing body in the country.*

*At the time of the election, 96% of Parliamentary seats were held by the Mongolian People's Revolutionary Party (MPRP), the party which had held power continuously for the past seventy-five years. When the ballots were counted, it was discovered that the communist MPRP had been voted out of power by a landslide victory of a coalition of democratic parties. The people of Mongolia had voted for change.*

*Some people waited in line for two to three hours to vote. There was an air of quiet determination in Ulaanbaatar: people had dressed up to go to their district schools to cast their ballots, and they took the process seriously. The food market was closed. The Department Store was on strike. Children still chased their hoops and flamed little piles of cottonwood fuzz in the streets, but there was a sense of something momentous quietly happening to the city. In the countryside, people rode their horses in to the somon centers. It was a remarkable national movement: the voter turnout was over 85%.*

*People voted overwhelmingly for a change in government: of a total of 76 seats, 52 are now held by Democrats who will be in power for the next four years. Narangerel was one of those voted into Parliament. She is 42 years old.*

I ran for office from District 72 in Ulaanbaatar. This district surrounds the Black Market, north of the city. It is an extremely poor area with a population of around 23,000 people, and it is made up only of gers: no houses, no buildings.

To campaign, I went to each of the six subdistricts, called *horool.* We had a truck, lined with flags and covered with posters and information. I gave speeches, using a microphone, and I met and talked with the people. We distributed fliers, moving through the narrow alleys among gers.

The four parties that make up the Democratic Coalition have a unified platform. I campaigned on that general platform, but emphasized in my campaigning that I alone could not effect change—that only if many of our coalition were elected could we succeed. Others did the same, and this, in part, is what led to such strong support.

Yes, it is true that keeping the campaign promises will not be easy. We know now what we are doing and how things should be, but reaching the goals will be difficult. Our coalition has enough brave people, enough willing people and well educated people, however, that I believe we will be successful. We will not go back. Of course the victory does not mean a green light—we anticipate considerable opposition along the way. But we have been, and we will continue to be, united in our approach. This is a peaceful revolution.

There are people who will fight us, in various ways. Our country had no alternative to the ruling party, the MPRP, for seventy-five years. This is the first time that the communists are the opposition in this country. It is natural that people will fight back with every weapon possible—there will be rumors, there will be crimes—not by leaders, of course, but in the background. And it will be good for us to have a strong opposition. After losing power, the MPRP will keep a very good check on us.

Mongolia is moving in a democratic direction, but we are still not democrats inside. We have made a start. Now we must keep the momentum going, to teach the people—no, teach is not the right word —to let the people see how democracy works.

I was born in Ulaanbaatar in the ger-district just to the east of the Black Market. It's a poor district, and I lived there until 1990. Only then did I move into an apartment. My parents were very normal people—father was a financial manager but he never joined the MPRP. This was unusual, for in those days everyone joined the Party. But he had a very ethical way of living, of behavior, of thinking. He never said anything about it, but we learned from his example. No bribes, for example, no taking from the left hand.

Of the seven children in my family, I am the youngest. I am now forty-two years old, and my parents had me when they were about my age. We had two cows and one horse and these provided us a little additional income. When I was about twelve or thirteen my father retired on his small pension. My mother didn't work—she stayed at home and looked after the children.

After secondary school here in Ulaanbaatar, I went to the Pedagogical Institute in Moscow. I am a Russian-language teacher by profession. I attended school in Moscow for five years, from 1971 to 1976, and while I was there I met many so-called dissidents. Some later left Moscow for the West, some stayed in the country. I made friends, and friends have been important to me—I keep the ties. At that time, it was a stimulating environment in Russia, underground poetry, underground papers.

After returning to Ulaanbaatar, I worked for ten years in the University. In 1986, I went to Moscow to get a PhD in linguistics. I never studied English formally—it's necessary, and I am now picking it up.

While in school, I started reading and educating myself. In Mongolia, it was as though we lived under a cup, in the dark. I first encountered information from the West in Russia. I read William Faulkner, Thornton Wilder, and so on, all through Russian translations. There was one film theater in Moscow which showed neo-realist Italian films, such as those by Antonioni, Visconti, Fellini, also films by Kurosawa and others. I watched movies, I went to museums, I exposed myself as much as possible to culture.

In 1989, I visited Prague and saw the Velvet Revolution occurring there. I was struck by this and by the contrast with Mongolia. We in Mongolia were so passive. I was envious of how they could organize, be active against communism. Then I heard about the creation of the Democratic Union in Ulaanbaatar, and when I heard that, I knew I must return to my country to participate. Several people were beginning to organize and I decided to join them.

I returned to Ulaanbaatar on December 28, 1989, the very day that the Social Democratic movement began. Following the start of the movement, we set up the Social Democratic Party in March, 1990.

At that time, as a PhD teaching in the University, I had an excellent position and a salary equivalent to that of a Deputy Minister. But five of us decided to leave the university and work full-time on political issues. I became Secretary of the Social Democratic Movement, then I was elected a member of the Social Democratic Party's Political Council. For six years we were fighting, openly. Before that, we had been fighting for many years in secret.

I have never married. My son was born in 1974. The father of my child was one of those friends I mentioned in Moscow—he left the Soviet Union in 1979 as a dissident, going to West Berlin where he lives now. He is a film director. In Russia, he married a Jewish woman and therefore was able to get out. When I graduated from school, he was in prison and it was impossible for us to marry; once I returned to Ulaanbaatar there was no way back. But we are very much in contact and I am a good friend of his wife as well. In 1979, he wanted to give his son his name, through the International Court. At that time, it would have been very dangerous for my son to carry the name of a Russian dissident living outside Russia. I said no. My son's name is therefore Narangerel Orgil—yes, it is unusual to have a woman's name instead of a man's in the father's place.

Perhaps it would have been better for me to be normal. Five children, staying home and cooking. But I doubt it. My principle is that if you do everything in accord with and to the extent of your feelings inside, and do not go against your innate sense of what is right and wrong, then you will be fine in the end. Those who are bright inside, not dark, can do a lot of things. Whoever is dark inside has eyes that are blind. One of my goals is to educate young people, and by this I do not mean giving them all degrees—many people with degrees are still dark inside. I was raised as an atheist but I believe in the power of good things. If you do good things, you will reach good goals.

# Relief map of Mongolia

Hovd
*(Chandaman culture)*

Lake Hovsgol

Ulaanbaatar

Gobi Altai Mountains
*(Tsagaan Agui)*

Gobi

*Mongolia: around two thousand miles across the country, east to west, population 2.4 million as of 1996. North of the country lies Buryatia, a part of Russian Siberia, and Lake Baikal, which is fed by the rivers of Mongolia. South of the country lies Inner Mongolia, one of the provinces of China.*